JOURNEY THROUGH LABRADOR

BY
BERNIE HOWGATE

(signature) Bernie Howgate

FOR A LADY WITH AN AGELESS PERSONALITY AND A MAGIC SMILE GOD BLESS

AUNT TINE
November 1st. 1933
November 26th. 1993

*The Travelling Man
Enterprises*

JOURNEY THROUGH LABRADOR
First Edition

WRITTEN
Bernie Howgate

EDITED
Bernie Howgate

COVER MAPS AND ILLUSTRATIONS
Bernie Howgate and Wendy Reger

PHOTOGRAPHS
Bernie Howgate

PUBLISHED
The Travelling Man Enterprises
General Delivery
Mud Lake
Labrador
A0P 1K0
CANADA

FIRST EDITION
1995

Printed in Canada

ISBN-0-9694419-1-6

COPYRIGHT © BERNIE HOWGATE

TALES OF A TRAVELLING MAN
by Bernie Howgate

Published by:
Travelling Man Enterprises
General Delivery
Mud Lake, Labrador,
Canada, A0P 1K0

Globe and Mail, May 9th, 1990

Howgate's book about an eight-year odyssey by bicycle around the world is a journey not only in the physical sense, but also through the earthy and sometimes disturbing subculture of the uprooted and the transient, who move slowly along roads not usually frequented by today's vacationers. His tale is a loamy mixture of obsevations and personal experiences, the most colourful of which unfolded on the Asian leg of his journey and range from the horror of a friend's rape in Singapore, to a dangerous journey through Nepal and life among the die-hard remnants of hippie communes in and around the Indian state of Goa.

Tales of a
Travelling
Man
By Bernie Howgate

EIGHT YEARS AROUND THE
WORLD ON A TEN SPEED BICYCLE
A Tremendous Reading
Adventure

Howgate has an ear for dialogue, a talent for writing and a better than-average illustrator's skills. He could use a good editor to focus and hone material that **has all the rough makings of a travel epic.**

THIS BOOK IS SELF PUBLISHED AND CAN ONLY BE PURCHASED BY MAIL ORDER. FOR A COPY PLEASE SEND $20:00 MONEY ORDER TO THE ABOVE MENTIONED ADDRESS.

CONTENTS

WINTER WALK

SUMMER KAYAK

MAP ILLUSTRATIONS

WINTER WALK

SUMMER KAYAK

"IS THERE ANYBODY OUT THERE"

I'm not religiouse by a long shot, but there are times, and tonight was one of them, when life skips onto another plane. Call it fate or just plain luck that blew me where it did. By all accounts, I should have been tucked away for the night in a cabin, instead I was outside. It was one of those glorious nights. A touch of frost kept the mosquitoes quiet. I could sit outside in peace and watch the sky go technicolour. Blood reds changed into deep purple then into the ink-black cloak of night. It was a childhood fantasy come true. My own observatory. The night was crystal clear. I traced the Big Dipper found the North Star and lined in the likes of Scorpio, Aries and Taurus the Bull. I must have tracked half a dozen satelites, named three planets and gazed in wonder at the Milky Way before the main event started. It began with a distant glow, like the far off haze of city lights. It slipped over the mountains, grew in brightness then exploded with life. Lines, tails, curls, it was everywhere. A curtain one minute, an old man's whiskers the next. It went from white to flourescent green to dull amber. For two hours the Northern Lights gave me a show, the likes of which I had never experienced before.

Chapter 1
A Chance Meeting

FOR THE LAST SIX WEEKS I'VE BEEN SUFFERing from lack of sleep. In my dreams I've just made camp. Suddenly a snow drift moves. It's a polar bear and it's coming in my direction. My brain says run, my legs say no. I don't know what happens next because at that point I always wake up.

For someone who is planning to leave on an eight month 2,500 mile solo trip of the Labrador Coastline and who has no experience of snow camping, let alone sea kayaking, dreams like this are understandable.

I can trace my present state back to 1980 and my first visit to Labrador. Since then I've criss-crossed North America, worked in New Zealand and Australia and spent years off the beaten track in Asia and Africa, but nothing has come close to the hospitality I experienced on Canada's remote east coast.

The seed of my coming trip took root a year ago with a chance meeting. Two travellers exploring new challenges over beers. During the evening the question of travel between Labrador's remote coastal communities surfaced. "There aren't any coastal roads", I told my friend. "Access in summer is by ferry only, and as for the winter, I just don't know." The more we talked the bigger the obstacles grew. Atlantic storms and arctic temperatures, not to mention the distances involved. "Sounds like your kind of place, Bernie". He was right. By the end of the evening, I'd given in to the idea and by the end of the week was making plans to go.

Saying and doing are poles apart. I spent weeks of research in libraries looking for travel books on the subject, but getting nowhere. Outside its mines, dam and low level flying, Labrador didn't seem to exist and, when I eventually dug up a book on the subject, the death of its expedition leader, 'Hubbard', didn't exactly fill me with enthusiasm. Then I got my first breakthrough. I dropped book research, turned to the source, and let my fingers do the digging.

One phone call to the RCMP detachment in Forteau, Labrador, and soon the doors of information opened. I was told it was feasible to travel by foot in winter from Red Bay to Goose Bay, and in summer the waters from Goose Bay to Nain were definitely navigable for kayaking.

First I addressed the winter portion of my trip from Red Bay. It would be impossible to live off the land and to pull three months' supply of provisions on a sled over 800 miles of frozen trail. The coastal map of Labrador is peppered with names. I was told most were summer fishing stations, some derelict and fewer still, year-round communities. I needed caches of food, but where could I send them? This time Canada Post came to the rescue. I devoted September to letter writing, sponsorship-hunting and food collection and by the end of the month, I had collected three months' supplies of dehydrated food and by mid-October five parcels had been addressed, marked 'Hold for pick-up', and posted to Port Hope Simpson, Charlottetown, Black Tickle, Cartwright and Rigolet. I then notified the postmasters in each settlement of my travel plans and by mid-November their arrivals were confirmed.

Next I turned my attention to clothes. I had been out in sub-zero conditions before, but cross-country skiing on marked trails, surrounded by fellow enthusiasts is a far cry from solo travel on barren windswept icefields.

All through October, I watched my budget drop as I put together a new wardrobe of heavy down, pile and gortex-lined clothes. In November, a cold snap found me camping in my back garden for three nights trying out new equipment, much to the amusement of neighbors.

In December, I flew to Vancouver to try out my new sea kayak. The first day out, I capsized. My escape underwater was flawless and my re-entry no problem. It was the frigid cold sea water that frightened me and this precipitated yet another burst of spending; before leaving the west coast, I had purchased a wet suit, a dry suit and every flotation device known to man.

Back home in Toronto another problem surfaced. I had originally planned to travel the traditional way in winter with a solid wooden sled and to camp in a high-wall canvas tent heated by a wood-fired tin stove. All through Christmas their combined weights played on my mind. I began asking everyone for advice. Speed was essential between settlements, but to cut back on weight would leave me at the mercy of the elements. In the end, I went with my gut feelings and by January had traded the heavier, but warmer, traditional equipment for a high-tech fibre glass sled, all season tent and arctic-rated, down-filled sleeping bag.

Now I'm ready. Everything is packed away in the basement. I have at least two of everything and more socks and gloves than I care to admit. No-one can say I'm not prepared. All I have to do now is start and that can't come too soon. Next stop, Red Bay.

Chapter 2
The Walking Man

THE GOOD NEWS, I MADE IT TO RED BAY. The bad news, I haven't moved in three days. For four nights I have been snow-bound at the foot of the Barrens in an emergency shelter. Every morning I've woken at 6:00 am., tuned to the C.B.C. weather forecast, heard the blizzard warning, then buried myself deep back into my sleeping bag. I'm on Labrador time.

Seven days ago I woke to the sweet smell of frying bacon. Outside the scene was a blanket of snow. A lone dog barked, then silence. The sun had not yet popped its head above the horizon and the coastal hills were still draped in their pre-dawn backdrop of gold and bronze. A still white desert covered the bay and dotted about its harbour, black box-like silhouettes topped by white smoke curled up as quietly as mist. For a split second I was in a dream. Then the sight of the thermometer earthed me.Minus 32deg. C. 'WELCOME TO LABRADOR'.

There is something about winter that brings life and symmetry to the North, and Red Bay is no different. Red Bay is literally the end of the road and was the start-off point for my 800 mile winter walk to Goose Bay. Nestled in a natural deep-water harbour at the end of the Straits of Belle Isle, this once great whaling port has dwindled in recent years to a scattered community of sixty families. I snook in under the cover of darkness, and now after a good night's sleep, I was ready to greet it.

Breakfast at the Laydens was a journey in itself: home-cooked bread, large-eyed eggs and generous portions of thickly sliced bacon.

My trip was put together on a shoe-string. I didn't

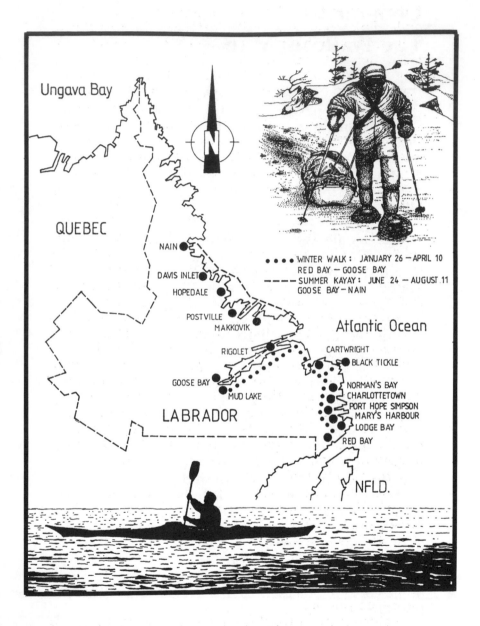

Ungava Bay

QUEBEC

NAIN

DAVIS INLET

HOPEDALE

POSTVILLE
MAKKOVIK

RIGOLET

GOOSE BAY
MUD LAKE

LABRADOR

Atlantic Ocean

CARTWRIGHT
BLACK TICKLE
NORMAN'S BAY
CHARLOTTETOWN
PORT HOPE SIMPSON
MARY'S HARBOUR
LODGE BAY
RED BAY

NFLD.

•••• WINTER WALK: JANUARY 26 – APRIL 10
RED BAY – GOOSE BAY
– – – SUMMER KAYAY: JUNE 24 – AUGUST 11
GOOSE BAY – NAIN

have the funds for hotels and anyway, it wasn't my style. I like to get under the surface of the areas I travel in, find out what makes people tick. Where else better to achieve this than in their homes? I found the Laydens through a friend of a friend. A long shot that turned up trumps. Yesterday they didn't know me from Adam; today I was being treated like a long-lost friend. That's how I like it. Instant karma. I needed a roof over my head and food in my belly. In return, I offered myself, an exchange of ideas and lifestyles. Today it was the Laydens and the family breakfast that put a human face on Labrador's famous hospitality.

My first morning brought with it a few surprises. News travels fast out here and I was an instant celebrity. "Are you the WALKING MAN?". I had a new title. Having just come from the melting pot of Toronto, it was strange meeting the same white faces. There wasn't a Chinese Restaurant or Curry House to be found anywhere. Then, just as I thought things would be boring, I tripped over my first dialect. "Jesus Lord, you're a crazy dumb boy". Words overlapped, sentences hung in the air, stalled, then snapped back like rubber bands. If I thought bilingualism stopped at the Quebec border, I was wrong. That morning the same questions followed me at every turn. "Why walk?", "Seen a doctor lately?","Want to buy a good ski-doo?" but the consensus of opinion was if I lived to cross the Barrens to Lodge Bay, then I'd be OK.

The cold at first was deceptive. It took your breath away. The slightest breeze stung, bones cracked, muscles ached and nose, toes and fingers felt as hard as lead. Walking was the only way to stay warm because to stop meant freezing. The crisp morning snow that crunched underfoot sang back by nightfall and no sooner had the sun set, than the evening stars peppered the sky.

After supper, I went for a walk. The stars were so clear I could almost touch them, and before I turned in for the night, the northern lights rainbowed over the horizon, splintered, then flew off in every direction like slow motion curtains of fire.

Day two started with a strip search of equipment. A timid pair of eyes attached to an oversized ski-doo suit was soon joined by an army of match-stick look alikes. My multi-coloured equipment spread out in the snow had stopped a group of school children in their tracks. Heads swivelled, eyes popped and soon nervous curiosity turned into a children's toy shop of new experience. It didn't take long before stares turned to touch. I didn't have the heart to refuse them and excited hands were soon pawing everything within striking distance.

I was in an editing mood. I wanted to lighten my load, yet by noon the only things I had discarded were my one and only book and an old pair of army breaches. I packed and unpacked my sled three times but, like a miser counting his money, everything stuck. One by one I ticked off my equipment and supplies:

> 1 x white gas stove c/w pot and pans
> 1 x petrol stove (spare)
> 1 x 1 litre fuel container (spare)
> 1 x 4 litre white gas
> 1 x 2 litre container full fat powdered milk
> 1 x 500 grams white sugar
> 1 x 50 tea bags
> 1 x 250 grams coffee
> 20 chocolate bars
> 6 candles and 6 match boxes
> 200 grams tobacco
> 20 days supply freeze dried food packets
> 4 pairs wool socks
> 2 pairs boot liners
> 1 x deerskin mukluks
> 1 x down-filled moccasins
> 1 x down-filled parka
> 1 x down insulated ski pants

2 x pair thermal underwear
2 x pair nylon shorts
2 x pair wool gloves
2 x pair nylon gloves
1 x gortex glove liners
2 x pile sweaters
1 x foam liner
1 x thermarest camp rest
1 x 5 star down filled sleeping bag rated -30 degC.
1 x gortex bivi sac
1 x binoculars
1 x fm/am/short wave digital radio
1 x 22/20 ga'over and under' shot gun and shells
1 x safety first aid kit
1 x flask
1 x 35mm camera
1 x compass
12 topographical maps scale 1:50,000
3 topographical maps scale 1:250,000

All that didn't include the clothes I stood in, the gortex wind jacket and overtrousers I would wear while walking, or my snow shoes, ski-poles, sled and harness. It made the mind boggle and all morning I shuffled the equipment around like playing cards until I was sufficiently confused and went in for lunch.

The afternoon held no respite. I was missing an important map of the Barrens. An S.O.S. went out. Soon the Laydens' phone was red hot and a steady stream of visitors appeared at their doorstep. It didn't take long to locate the missing link and before nightfall, the final piece of the jigsaw - a detailed map of Chateau Ponds - had been tracked down.

By late evening, the kitchen was filled with the chatter of local knowledge, maps were being pored over, routes argued about, and compass readings written down. I've never been one to spoil a trip by knowing too much, so I revelled in their animated descriptions of the trail ahead. By all accounts, the route below the Barrens was hard packed and easy to follow, but fresh snow could alter that completely; as for the route markers, they weren't exactly neon street signs. The slightest wind, I was told, could lead to 'white outs' and the razor sharp cold to a frosty death. Not exactly uplifting, but by the end of the evening it was magic.

Next day, I turned my attention to repair work. I'm not a handyman-changing light bulbs is my limit so when Leslie's cousin offered to repair my fibre glass sled broken in transit, I left it with him.

That night I was invited to a 'Pot Luck Supper'. The venue was the community centre. Each family was to bring some food and by the time we got there, tables were full to overflowing. There was caribou stew, caribou pie, moose steak, braised duck, chicken casserole, jigs dinner, peas pudding and every variation of wild berry pie you could think of. There wasn't a spice to be tasted. Here was good wholesome food made by people with simple tastes and quantity, not quality, ruled the night.

The tables were set in two straight lines; men at one side, women at the other. The vicar said grace, then it was on to the serious business of eating. My first helping went down in double quick time, the second followed without missing a beat, but after the third, I threw in the towel and staggered home like a pregnant pig.

It was my last morning and I was doing the tourist rounds with my camera: pyramid of driftwood; sculptured snow drift; children slapping a puck around and yet another group skiing. The initial two-way suspicion had melted. After three days I had become part of Red Bay's furniture and was having a rare old time. Doors stayed open, ski-doos continued on their merry way and I could stain the snow without embarrassment. By mid-morning, I had recorded bread fresh from the oven, a fox being skinned and a brace of ducks plucked ready for the pot. Then a cloud of steam captured my attention. It was washing day and I climbed a wood pile for a better view. A red shirt fluttered, cracked then froze like a board to the line. Snap, snap, I was zooming in for a closer look when a stick cracked. The glue of ice broke underfoot and a chain reaction moved me sideways. An arm went out, my hip jerked. Suddenly the sky arched. A rainbow of clouds flew by, then I kissed the snow. It went everywhere. Up my sleeves, down my neck. What a sight I made, head down like an ostrich with my ass in the air. Embarrassment wasn't the word for it. I'd been spotted, and within minutes I was holding a piping hot mug of tea surrounded by a kitchen filled with female laughter.

By nightfall, I was shooting across bay ice. I was late for supper at the Laydens and this was all the excuse my ski-doo driver needed. Zero to 60 in milliseconds. My heart somersaulted then fell back into my boots. One bump later my sex life almost ended. Was this the fast lane or an out of body experience? The question was never answered. We hit a snow drift and my brain scrambled. The next I remembered was eating. Could life be more exciting?

Later that evening, my sled was returned. Repaired, it was as good as new. Tomorrow the long slow march would begin. I kept repeating the dangers in my head. Blizzards, frostbite, bad ice, tent fires and angry polar bears. The list was endless. I was penetrating the belly of the travel beast and it made my stomach turn. I crawled to the bathroom, stopped at the door, pulled myself together and returned to bed. Did everyone go through this before an expedition, or was it just me? Back in bed, my mind raced, crashed, then ground to a halt. Somewhere exhaustion took over and the next I remembered, it was 5:00 a.m. Time to get up.

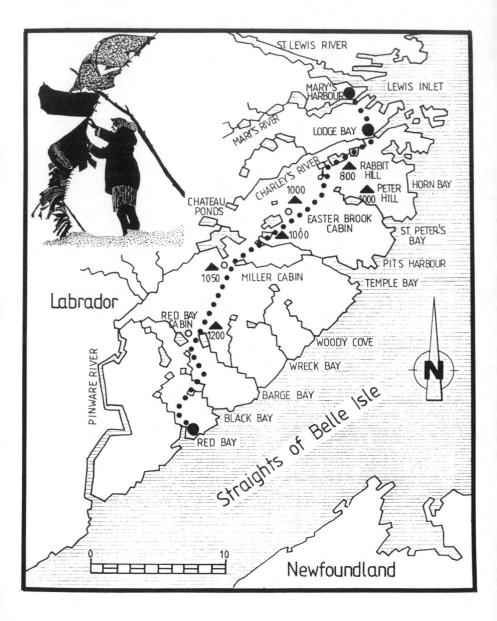

Chapter 3
The Barrens

IFOUND PHYLLIS IN THE KITCHEN MAKING
sandwiches. She'd already cut one loaf of bread
and was in the process of cutting another. She'd
never say it to my face, but from the first moment we
met, she'd tried her best to fatten me up. Meat, meat
and more meat. There was enough bologna, ham,
and caribou to feed an army. "Don't want you starv-
ing to death, Bernard". Heavy, fatty and to be digest-
ed thoroughly. A vegetarian wouldn't last long here.
I thought about telling her, but kept it to myself.

I slipped out of the front door into a sleeping
world. It was 7:00 am. Behind the house a woodpile
stood like a ghostly teepee and behind that, illuminated by a grey and amber haze, were the dark hills I
would have to cross. The morning weather forecast
was for clear skies with a low of minus 28 deg. C. and
a high of minus 16 deg. C. The air was crisp and a
fresh dusting of snow sparkled and crunched like
broken styrofoam underfoot. The plan was for Leslie
to take me and the sled to the outskirts of Red Bay.
Apparently, the trails in and around the community
were so numerous that hitting the right one in the
grey light of morning would be as difficult as looking
for a needle in a haystack, and I wasn't too keen at the
thought of getting lost on my first day. I said my
goodbyes, loaded the sled onto Leslie's wooden
komatik and then straddled the ski-doo for the ten
minute ride out of town.
"Look, Bernie, take my axe".
It wasn't the first time someone had warned me
about travelling in the country without one. "I'd
rather take an axe than a gun anytime, Bernie". It's an
unwritten law in these parts not to leave home with-

out one. Deep down, I knew Leslie was right, but the thought of extra weight coloured my judgement. "Thanks, but no thanks". We shook hands, but said nothing. Then just before leaving he shouted. "Don't forget to call me when you get to Lodge Bay. People know the 'Walking Man' is coming". I turned into his laughter, then he was gone.

There is nothing like the real thing to sober you up. Back at the Laydens, a line drawn on a map looked easy to follow and a description of a hard-packed ski-doo trail sounded easy to walk on. The first leg to the Barrens by all accounts should be a piece of cake. I didn't have to worry about bad ice, polar bears, or getting lost. "Just follow the ski-doo tracks." So much for the armchair advisers. First, who wants to chase a boring trail when a short-cut over virgin snow looks so inviting? I do, well I did, but I don't now. Ski-doo trails, as I found out the hard way, are like ice bridges over a quicksand of powdered snow where one wrong step can leave you waist deep. And as for those easy landmarks, the ones that beg a compass reading, they all looked the same. It would be a case of two steps forward and one step back until I got my bearings and walking legs.

My body didn't start complaining until noon. Some muscles were going into shock while others had gone on strike. Who could blame them? The surface was forever changing, predictable as a pavement one minute and like a skating rink the next. They were ideal ankle buckling conditions. Then there was my harness, that super-sophisticated device I had converted from a piece of mountain climbing equipment. It sent shock waves round my shoulders, and no amount of adjustment stopped it. All morning, I heard from muscles I never knew existed. In fact, the one thing I had braced myself for, frostbite, never materialized. I was sweating like crazy. Within the first hour my body climbed the comfort zone from chilled to boiling and I was constantly stopping to unzip, peel and strip off surplus insulation.

After four miles of relatively flat going, I came to the 'T' Junction everyone had warned me about. "Keep to the right, boy. The left trail goes to the wood cut". At first I was confused. It's not that I don't know my left from my right, but the left trail definitely looked the most travelled and it wasn't until I saw a bright red fuel container nailed to a branch that I knew with certainty which trail to take.

Twenty minutes later I was at the top of a rise when suddenly the wind struck. It didn't creep up; there was no hint, no clouds, no valleys to flute down, so it took me completely unawares. One second I was drinking in the scene, the next deafened by it. Immediately,my fingers hardened.The wind searched through clothes, froze sweat on impact and sucked my breath away. Toes pointed, joints stiffened, even my hair took on a life of its own. Luckily the trail nose-dived into a sheltered valley, but I should have been more cautious. One second I was grounded at the top, the next airborne going down it. The experience was amazing. A free fall into childhood memories until an exposed branch spoiled it. A cord snapped. My sled's canvas cover opened and equipment spewed out in all directions.

I now found myself following a mini roller coaster of brooks, ponds and steep banks. I was very tired. The morning's climb had drained me like a leaky cup, and on hearing a ski-doo coming, found the excuse needed to take a break. It was a teacher from Red Bay. He'd come out with his son to check on my progress. We exchanged greetings and small talk. I was still within spitting distance of Red Bay; still there not here. They stayed only five minutes, but on leaving they took with them the last pieces of home. My bridges were burnt. I was now truly on my own and for the first time since Toronto, I felt the full weight of the walk ahead.

Invariably when things go wrong it's the sum

total of the small things that add up to accidents and feeling sorry for yourself is a main ingredient. I'd rested in the teacher's visit for too long. I was cold. I wanted to get up but my eyes were riveted to the can of Coke he'd left. I couldn't let it go. I don't even like Coke, but a gift is a gift and not to be wasted. I snapped it open, took a mouthful and .... "OUCH"... One gram of prime lip froze on touch and tore off. Five minutes later I bloodied my nose in a fall, and five minutes after that my harness broke.

I was still climbing at 2:00 p.m.. High hills on either side tapered in; dark blue, tier upon tier, with long uneven ridges. It took me the better part of the afternoon to ascend the valley. Below, the view opened out onto three large tree-lined ponds and beyond, half hidden by a blue haze, were the treeless Barrens.

I just started to cross the second pond when the sight of smoke broke into my mood. It was Red Bay Cabin. My steps gained more purpose. I soon crossed into a fresh ski-doo track, followed it across to the third pond, and there at the edge of a clearing, was the cabin. I was now singing to myself. All the self-doubt, the ifs and buts of the day's adventure, were history. I arrived just ahead of the afternoon sun and by the time I downed my first mug of tea, its rays were emptying down the invisible corridors of the trail ahead. Again, people had gone out of their way to help and if the cabin's fire and its owner's friendly conversation were signs of things to come, my travel worries would be halved.

I was into my fourth cup of tea when the weather forecast started. "A blizzard warning is in effect for the South East Coast, the Straights of Belle Isle and Central Labrador." Moncton had been buried under eight feet of snow and by all accounts the same blizzard would hit Labrador by morning.

My watch thermometer had jumped 10 degrees since supper. Anywhere else but Labrador such jumps would herald a heat wave, but here they say,

'WHEN WINTER WARMS UP THERE'S GONNA BE SNOW'. Would it snow tonight or tomorrow? It was no use worrying, I'd know soon enough.

After my friends left, I set about exploring. My maps showed three cabins between Red Bay and Lodge Bay and ten more between Mary's Harbour and Norman's Bay. They were all built to act as emergency shelters for the coastal ski-doo trails. Sub-zero temperatures in Labrador can be unforgiving, especially if you're caught out in a storm, but as the wall graffiti suggested, this cabin had seen more than its share of steamy nights. I was told that the cabins varied from the 'Swiss Family Robinson' all-inclusive, to the spartan 'Flintstone' type. Built at twenty mile intervals along the trail, they were life-savers. By all accounts I should be outside in my tent tonight roughing it, but at this rate, if the information was correct, I wouldn't have to put up the tent until past Norman's Bay, 200 mile to the north.

Besides the essential stove and well stocked wood pile, the cabin was a veritable pharoe's tomb of survival goodies. Shelves were filled to overflowing. I counted over fifty tea bags, one tin of coffee and half a jar of sugar, as well as ample supplies of candles and matches. There were pots and pans of every description and a miss-match supply of cutlery. Sitting and dining was all in one, while above, accessed by a step ladder, was the open loft. Up there I found two sleeping bags wrapped in plastic, a floor covered in mattresses and a packet of 'TROJANS' of dubious value. One wall, decorated with hooks, held everything from bucksaw to brush and at the base of another was the wood pile. Pride of place went to the Red Cross Survival Kit. Inside, I found enough bandages, tape and magic healing ointments to both mummify and revive a whole family and going by the well stocked container of flares, enough fire power to bring down a satellite. There was also your standard compass, thermal blankets and dehydrated food. It was an easy setting, a nice balance of no-non-

sense supplies and homely furniture with an atmosphere that invited occupancy any time, especially in
bad weather.

The heat was now rising and the cabin's thick lining of interior frost started to melt. At first it kept to
the walls, but by supper had reached the loft and by
bed time was raining in from the ceiling. I thought
about erecting the tent inside, but the only available
floor space was too close to the stove heat. In the end
I found myself bedding down under the kitchen table
to escape the thaw.

Sleep comes quickly after a hard day's work. I
was still drunk with excitement. My first day and still
in one piece. I was now snug inside the down-filled
world of my sleeping bag. Every so often the hiss of
thawing ice striking the stove woke me, but by 10:00
o'clock the low groans of wind nudged me into sleep.

That first morning I had to jump-start my body.
The fire had gone out and my breath steamed. I
awoke to the same whistling sounds of wind that had
put me to sleep. Through the window a murky white
was the only sign of daylight, but when the door
nearly ripped off its hinges, I knew the blizzard had
arrived. They would be no progress today and none
tomorrow if it hadn't run its course. By mid-morning
the snow was pushing its way up the steps and by
afternoon I was digging myself out. To fill in the
day's empty spaces, I turned my attention to packing
arrangements. Yesterday I almost lost fingers to the
cold while searching for items in the sled, so today I
decided to pull everything out and start again. I had
three duffel bags. Non- essentials were packed away
in the two larger ones; extra clothes, toiletries and
sleeping bag in one; tent, thermal mats, spare stove,
extra boots and camera in the other. They were both
secured under the sled's canvas top cover, while the
third bag, containing my food, stove and flask for the
day's refreshment would be attached with my gun by
bunji cords on top of the sled for easy access. I was

pulling over 120 lbs. but if yesterday was any indication, windswept surfaces posed no problem. What it would be like after fresh snow, however, was anyone's guess.

For dinner, I fried four of my bread sandwiches and drank gallons of tea. Then I turned my attention to another job. I've never had problems with zippers before, but then I've never had to negotiate a toilet stop in windchill conditions of minus 60 deg. C. Trying to pull down a two centimeter zipper while wearing heavy mitts was as bad as asking a brain surgeon to operate in boxing gloves. I needed to make the zipper catch bigger. I found the answer in some thin cord brought along for extra lacing; I spent the next hour attaching small loops of it to every pocket, fly, vent and tent zipper, and then practised with mitts on until I was confident the idea worked.

Boy, how time flies when you're having fun! I spent the whole day picking away at my equipment and with the exception of calls of nature, I'd not stuck my head out of the door. I could still hear the angry demons outside, but inside it was 100 degrees in the shade. Apart from the small drifts of powdered snow by the door I could have been in Florida. The cabin was now bone dry and that night found me sleeping in the loft. I didn't want a replay of the frosty morning so to ensure that I woke up when the fire needed more wood, I slept not inside, but on top of my sleeping bag.

Next day the blizzard was no better and by the third day I was getting claustrophobic. The weather hadn't abated and the forecast was for more of the same. I was now searching for things to do. My gun was spotless, my harness now felt like an old glove and I had combed through my equipment at least a dozen times. Patience doesn't come easy to a city boy. The action man in me had been doused out like a dead squid by the storm. I now spent twice as much time inside my sleeping bag than out. By the fourth day, I was climbing the walls. The wood pile wasn't even dented and with the exception of snow collection for melting purposes, I was a prisoner of inactivity. Each minute was a year and the continual roaring engines of the blizzard made my head ache.

Then something snapped. One moment I was looking at my snow shoes and the next I was outside wearing them. The cold kicked like a mule and the snow stung like pins, but it felt great. At last I was doing something.

Three days and the geography had changed. The steps up to the cabin had disappeared and the only thing that marked the outside woodpile was the top half of a lone stick. Drifts leaned everywhere. All trees were stripped, wind-hardened snow stuck like glue and all footprints and ski-doo tracks were buried. The lake below was just an eerie blur and ahead the trail to the Barrens was furrowed in deep eddies of snow. This was my first experience with snow shoes. I had been too shy in Red Bay. Now, unseen, I could find my snow legs. For twenty minutes, I stumbled about from hard crust to powder, tripping over my edges, standing on my tails and doing back strokes with my hands. A rhythm was coming slowly. It wasn't text book style, but it was working. The tree-lined trail abruptly ended two hundred yards from the cabin and half a dozen steps later a blast of wind decked me. Lesson over, I retraced my way, but before the cabin came into view my footprints were gone.

My spirits soared at the next radio forecast: clear skies and lower temperatures. With a bit of luck I could leave tomorrow. But where to? If the tracks had been covered below the Barrens then there wasn't a hope in hell of finding them. What if I got lost? The embarrassment of it. I could just see the headlines: 'WALKING MAN LOST ON FIRST DAY.' My maps hadn't yet given up their secrets. I hadn't quite mastered compass reading. I could take bearings from known landmarks, but I was a long way from matching contour lines with solid objects.

I took out tomorrow's map and made a few notes;

0 - 3 ml N.E.   - Steep gradient, hill on right
3 - 5 ml E.   - Round hill, cross small pond
5 - 6 ml N.E.   - Drop down to large pond
6 - 7 ml   - To brook
7 - 9 ml N.E.   - Rise to high plateau. hill on left
9 - 13 ml N.E.   - Follow ridge to Miller Cabin

The decision to leave was made as soon as I put pencil to paper. I pulled out all surplus food, spare stove and camera, then broke down my gun and repacked everything into the small duffel bag. The idea was to lighten my load. I didn't want to be caught out on the Barrens for one minute longer than was necessary. I would give the bag to the first ski-doo that passed, for pick-up later in Lodge Bay. I felt much better. Tomorrow couldn't come quickly enough. All that was required now was the weather's co-operation.

I woke to perfect conditions. The sky was clear and there was not a hint of wind. I fired up the stove, had a light breakfast, filled my flask with coffee, then replayed the lost and injured scenario one last time in my head. I started by ticking off the backups: first aid kit, compass, maps and matches. The Barrens offer little protection against the elements so I decided at the last moment to bring my gortex bivi-sac. I may get caught out in a storm. One man igloo tents when erected and pinned down are as, steady as rocks, but if they catch the wind when you're not in them, good-bye tent. Then there was my planned escape route. If lost, I would turn west, follow the Barrens natural drainage system, pickup the Pinware River and follow it back down to the sea.

I was on the trail by 8:00 a.m.. I had on my snow shoes, but immediately I crossed the tree line, took them off. In just ninety minutes I had covered two miles, climbed five hundred feet and experienced surface changes from powder, to wind hardened, to a polished surface of frost under yesterday's gale force winds. Walking conditions were ideal - just the right balance of friction under foot, yet glazed enough for my sled to glide freely.

One hour later the landscape opened like a book. To the north and west the scenery rolled away in all directions. Smooth curved hills rose and fell like white pin cushions and to the east a shortened horizon, blocked off by low ridges, opened without warning to views of a streaming Atlantic.

It was no coincidence that nature had been shaved off at the knee caps. The slightest breeze pickedup like a runaway express train. Twisted trees hid behind boulders and a few stunted ones clung to life down shallow ridges. I'd been told that here on the Barrens the wind always blows and surface snow constantly moves. With this in mind I always kept one eye on the trail ahead and the other on the weather above.

By 11:00 a.m. I'd crossed the pond but by noon I was lost. Stopping to readjust the sled cords, I'd taken off my heavy mitts only to watch helplessly as the wind stole one. I was still hooked to my sled and by the time I released the harness clip, put on my snow shoes and chased the mitt down, I had lost sight of the next marker. With no visible ski-doo tracks to follow, the trail markers were my only life-line. They came in all shapes and sizes: pyramids of sticks, painted boulders, wood nailed to trees, old gas tanks strung from branches and even beer cans. I kept checking my map, but at this elevation one hill looks very much like another and with few trees, ponds or ridges, definition is non-existent.   At first I thought this good practice; the trail couldn't be far away. But after ten minutes of further compass reading my fingers went to sleep. I spent five minutes beating them across my shoulder and putting them under my armpits, but most of all I took the time to clear my head. The temperature had been dropping all day. I was over one thousand feet and with the wind chill factor it must have been under minus 50 deg. C. Fear is your worst enemy when you travel alone. You can't make allowances for acts of God, but you can reduce the odds against the human ones. I climbed a ridge, took out my binoculars and prayed. Hills dropped away in all directions, white on white. My eyes travelled 360 deg. not once but twice. I was getting desperate but then a man-made shape caught my attention. A mound of stones. I was back on track.

Within sight of Miller Cabin I was passed by two ski-doos. At first they didn't see me. I was off the trail taking a short cut. Shouting would have been a waste of time. Ski-doos have the same droning noise a motorbike has minus a muffler and at full throttle a pack of them could be mistaken for the 'INDY 500' on race day, but today the gods were smiling. The ski-dooers saw the trail I made chasing down the lone mitt and when realizing I hadn't made the cabin, doubled back for a second look. I now had the opportunity to off-load excess baggage, but my first question had them falling about laughing.

"Could you drop my bag off at Mrs Pye's house ?"

"Pye, you want us to leave the bag with Mrs. Pye? Which Mrs. Pye? They're all Pyes in Lodge Bay." My friend then reeled off a list of Pyes whose relationship to each other could have come straight out of the Old Testament; A beggat B, son of C, daughter of D. First, second, and third cousins. I couldn't help but laugh, and after a short deduction, the detective in him brought forth an answer.

"It's Margaret you want, her cousin Sandra is the one you spoke to. Just ask for Maggie, her house is at the bottom of the hill as you get into town."

I got a shock at Miller Cabin. Six junks of wood and not a dead twig in sight. I needed a fire badly, one that would last past the first brew-up and more importantly dry my damp clothes. Today I'd committed the cardinal sin, sweating. I didn't realize it until the ski-doos came and before they left I was shivering. A thin layer of frost coated my windbreaker and balls of ice stuck to the fabric of my pile sweater. Even my gloves and boot liners were damp. Everything had to come off. I stripped, dried myself in baby powder and changed in double quick time.

The cold made me careless. I was doing three things at once - fire tending, cooking and laundry -. then just as I thought things were under control, a burning smell set off a chain reaction that ruined a mitt, blistered my hand and decorated the floor with my evening meal. A mit fell from hook to stove. I panicked; moved too quickly, slipped, hit the stove with my hand and my arm did the rest. It wasn't even dark before I turned in. The fire had gone out. I felt sick. A dull pain flared up, then exploded as if under spontaneous combustion. I had cold sweats, fever and shakes, but by morning they had cleared and all I had to show for the night's adventures was a small purple blister.

I woke to a bone-chilling coldness. It was minus 28 deg. C. but felt much colder. Inside and out my nose was raw. A thin film of ice formed where my head had been and my hair was tinted with frost. Breath froze on exit and as soon as I moved, heat vacuumed out of my sleeping bag. The twilight hours before sunrise were always the worst. The thought of getting up was almost as painful as reality. My sleeping bag was rated to minus 35 deg. C. Although cold on entry, my body heat warmed it quickly and I only wore thermal underwear out of comfort not warmth, but once inside, wild horses couldn't drag me out.

To save precious heat I stored socks, mitts and gloves by my toes, but being able to dress inside the sleeping bag was a different matter. A blind Yogi would have been the ideal person. Everything was done by touch. There was never quite enough room to bend or twist. It was an art, but one I would have to learn more out of necessity than choice. But getting dressed was the easy part; at that stage my foot was just testing the waters. Lighting the white gas stove under candlelight, with only nylon gloves for protection, was like being thrown into the deep end and if that wasn't enough to glue me in bed, I then needed a touch of sado-masochism to pack a sled away, with its accompanying cord adjustments, while my blood was still thick enough to curdle.

Today I paid particular attention. A good start was essential. Miller Cabin was smack dab in the middle of the Barrens. It would now be just as easy to go forward as back. Susan's fax about the dangerous Barrens hadn't gone unnoticed. Outside, the morning sky looked sickly. Low clouds hid the sun and the bare cold hills were a depressing shade of grey. The forecast called for strong north-east winds by the afternoon and a 'WINDCHILL' warning was in effect. Before starting I took a bearing on the Fox Harbour radio beacon. I only took two minutes, but that's all it took for whiskers to icicle and as I bent down, drops fell from nose to knee, freezing on impact. My initiation to the Labrador winter was taking its toll. So far I'd stayed in cabins and I was heading for another. I dreaded the thought of being caught outside. Putting up a tent was still an abstract idea. I hadn't come to grips with the cold yet and I was beginning to think I never would.

Things went from bad to worse. I set off at 8:00 a.m., chasing yesterday's ski-doo tracks, but by 10:00 a.m. I was lost. For two hours I walked a tight rope, hanging on to the trail, falling off and getting back on again. Not once did I check my map, or take my compass out. All the time my eyes locked onto ski-doo tracks, memorizing directions, working out angles and trying to fill in the blanks the new snow drifts blotted out. This time the trail came to a full stop. The tracks ahead disappeared at the bottom of two identical gullys. Last night's wind had plugged the bottom of both under tons of snow. This wasn't a hiccup, this was a major problem. If I chose the wrong gully the chances were I would be putting up my tent sooner rather than later. I retraced my steps, checked the track angles, took an educated guess, then went to to the right. Half way up the gully the tip of my snow shoes caught a submerged object and down I went. No problem - wrong - big problem. I couldn't make up from down. Snow and sky fused. Above, the dull afternoon made a perfect match for the gully and everything turned white. I searched for lines but the more I concentrated the dizzier I got. I tried to stand up. My mind had nothing to push off from and my legs reacted accordingly, and down I went. Twice I replayed the incident. Then my eyes took hold of a branch and the picture returned. Once again I was on track. Now the only obstacle that came between me and my descent of the Barrens was a frozen waste called Chateau Ponds.

Here I found ski-doo tracks going off in all directions. I was told that the one-mile long pond ahead was notorious for white-outs and many a local got lost for hours crossing it. Again, yesterday's wind had wiped the surface clean. I was searching the opposite shore line for a diamond shaped ski-doo trail marker that I knew existed. My map showed the trail existing above a creek to the north east, so I set my compass and headed out on its bearings.

I'd not gone far when I heard a whining noise. I looked up, but saw no plane. In front the scene was still clear. I took out my compass, checked the direction, then returned it to my pocket. All this time the noise grew louder. Visibility was still excellent, then a burst of wind changed everything. To the north a curtain of white rubbed out the shore line. I was caught out in a wind storm and there was nothing to do except brace myself. Within seconds the cloud of snow hit. My vision shut down. Everything turned foggy white and I couldn't hear myself think. Snow particles were getting everywhere. It was like dust; it got in my eyes, up my nose and down my throat. Eddies of cold air freeze-dried sweat and my clothes literally ballooned under its pressure. The only thing I knew for certain was that my feet were grounded. I

dug out the compass. I only had my mitts off for a
few seconds, but my fingers froze. Every so often, I
dropped to my knees, doubled up and put my hands
down my pants for heat. My eyes were watering and
soon my left eye froze shut. For the next ten minutes
I crawled along on automatic pilot. My eye was riveted to the compass and I didn't dare turn away
from the wind. I don't know if it was naivete or the
compass that kept me going, but finally the wind
died and the ski-doo marker appeared. For a whole
minute my body jerked with relief. I was crying,
happy to be alive. Then I was earthed by the sight of
two heavy mitts dangling from cords attached to my
sleeves. I still held my compass, but my hands would-
n't release it. I was wearing only a pair of nylon
gloves. I could see my hands but my brain couldn't
talk to them. They were lifeless. They wouldn't
clench and try as I could they wouldn't fold up in my
pockets either. Frost bite, amputation. I tried to block
out the thought, but couldn't. The only sign of life
was a feeling of pins and needles. Then I remembered the snow. Pain. I never thought I'd live to crave
it. Red hot pain and the more I washed them in the
snow the deeper it went. I was lucky. A pair of thin
nylon gloves had saved my fingers and by the time
my blood returned to normal a dull throb was the
only reminder of my fright.

I now threw caution to the wind. All trails led
down. I didn't want to stop until Easter Brook Cabin
and a hot fire. I could now see the coastal hills and
deep inlets blanketed in trees. By early afternoon I'd
reached the tree line. I was sweating again and short
stops chilled me to the bone. Occasionally I'd wander
off course. Once I landed in a concealed snow-covered spruce thicket up to my waist, but mostly the
trail markers kept me out of trouble. Just before
Easter Brook I met up with two ski-dooers. I asked all
the usual questions. 'Where, how long and what's
the latest weather forecast?' Then it was their turn.
"You walked over the Barrens?" Their tone was a

mixture of crazy disbelief and congratulations. "Why?" I couldn't answer that one and fortunately they didn't press it. "Can we give you a lift?" They were out hunting partridge and going in the opposite direction, but a change in plans would be no problem. I explained, as best I could, my plans of walking all the way to Goose Bay and my visits to settlements en route. Immediately an invitation for Lodge Bay followed, but I had already a place to stay. "Well, can we help?" All thoughts of partridges were put on hold. They promised to leave a track to follow, described the route to the cabin, said they would light me a fire and check the wood, then left before their hospitality registered.

By late afternoon the sight of smoke made all the day's trials and tribulations worth it. Nestled in a sheltered valley between fern trees, Easter Brook Cabin was everything I could hope for - small, cozy and rustic, and the freshly cut junks of wood left for me inside spoke volumes for the two young men I'd met earlier.

I was soaking wet but I didn't care. The Barrens were history. I jumped through their hoops and come of age. That night I watched the icy stars behind a Disney World of futuristic shapes. Cold pressed in through the windows. The temperature outside had plummeted to minus 34 deg. C. but inside I was lost in luxury.

I was up and ready before 6:00 a.m. My adrenalin was pumping and I wanted to vent it before my mind changed. Last night I had seriously considered staying in Easter Brook an extra day. Back in Toronto I would have given my right arm for a weekend in the cabin. The whole scene brought back memories of long weekends, bedside slippers and lazy snoozes. Above, the sky was royal blue with just a hint of gold, while below, Easter Brook sliced through a piece of nature that begged more than just a second glance. I wanted to play in the snow, unwind and recharge my batteries. I deserved it, but I didn't want people in Lodge Bay worrying about me either. Somehow a feeling of shared ownership was creeping into my trip. Everyone I met embraced it. I received advice and encouragement from day one, and the inevitable open invitations like, "You must stay at my brother's when you get to Cartwright and drop-in anytime, boy," were coming thick and fast. I was quickly becoming public property. People cared. They were seeking me out, and I didn't want to disappoint or endanger them by taking stupid risks. I was expected in Lodge Bay and I knew they would worry if I was overdue. I didn't want to be the cause of a search party. It was one thing to court danger on your own, but unforgivable to lead someone else into it. I knew I would have to rein in my freewheeling ways and if that meant missing out on a peaceful day, it was a small price to pay for the hospitality I was encounting.

What a difference a day makes. Yesterday I thought pulling a sled was the world's worst form of torture, today the healthiest. Within thirty minutes I was stripped down to my thermals. Soon the tree line had swallowed me up. I now followed a trail packed solid and cut in deep ski-doo tracks through fresh snow. I was stepping down through a narrow wood-cut. Pools of light flooded open plateaus and crossing Peter's Pond was like walking on stardust. I was making great time. The harsh outlines of early morning were now smooth, and the sun was all heat.

Rounding Rabbit Hill I walked straight into a raw sea breeze. I was back in the open. Below, the valley basement was filled with interconnecting frozen ponds of white, and I could trace them all the way through the blanket of ferns to a window of sea ice. I was home and dry. There was a spring in my step that even the constant flipping over of my sled couldn't dull and for the first time in days my stomache rumbled to the thought of home cooked food.

After eight miles, I came onto the groomed ski-doo trail. I was now walking down a two lane highway centered by a ridge of snow. Civilization was just around the corner and when two ski-doos passed without stopping, I knew for sure. By early afternoon the countdown was on. 5 miles to go, 4,3,2,1.

"I'm here."

I walked straight into baking day at the Pyes'. "Come in, boy, don't bother with your boots." Instant recognition. My frozen whiskers gave me away, and Margaret's words greeted me like a ray of sunshine.

Chapter 4
Lock up your fridges Bernie's here

F RESH BREAD WAS IN THE AIR. I DIDN'T need a second invitation and when the food hit the table all thoughts exited my head. I had eyes only for the steaming caribou stew, and a belly to match. I had breezed into the Pyes' house, but they hadn't missed a beat. As with the Laydens in Red Bay I slipped into their world with the ease of an extended family member and outside the first cup of tea everything was offered on a help yourself basis.

I topped up my tanks, unzipped, then lay back to vegetate. Thirty minutes later I was steaming. A pungent smell stained the air. It wasn't caustic, it neither nipped the nose buds nor blocked its passages. It smelled all too familiar; even the dog knew it. My pores had opened. Internal combustion caused by food and heat combined to peel off a seven day layer of sweat. Bad breath is one thing, it can be deflected or expunged with a quick mouth wash, but body odour is like a second skin. There's no escaping it and, with a 360 deg. striking angle, doesn't leave much space for conversation. I shouldn't have worried, Margaret had experienced it all before. Sweat and dirt are part and parcel of life on the coast. Image is still a word in her home, not a lifestyle. When you rub shoulders with your neighbors each day, life is bound to catch you with your trousers down sooner or later.

Margaret was in complete command of the situation. She had no doubt gone through the exercise countless times with her children and while I was snoozing in the living room, she put two huge pans on to boil.

I was now refreshed. The bath worked wonders on my body. I even looked human and for the first

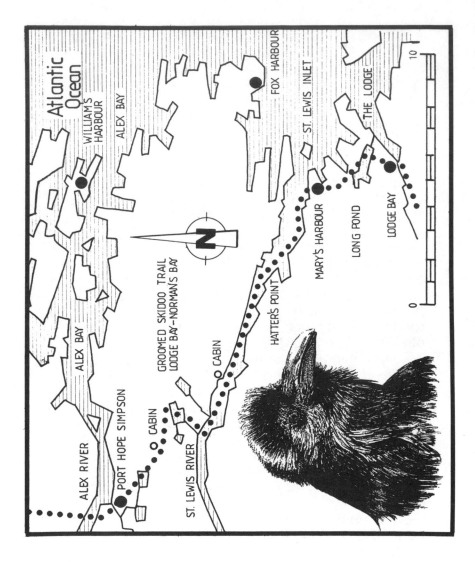

time the dog wagged its tail. Only my stomach complained. For seven days I had abused it with a combination of freeze-dried sandwiches and dehydrated food. Margaret's dinner reawakened its zest for the good life and now it craved a second fix. I hovered around her kitchen like a thief in the night, not knowing what to touch, if I was being watched, or if the alarm bells would go off. "Would you like to join us? We're going to the community centre. There's a Pot Luck Supper tonight." Two in one week. Somebody up there likes me.

I'm still an amateur when it comes to body language and household decorum. At the Laydens, I forgot where the toilet was. Too many doors and not enough light switches. I ended up outside. So when I got up to answer the 'call' at the Pyes I was prepared. Everything went to plan. The door opened silently. I turned left. The toilet was first door on the left down the hallway. Suddenly the floor disappeared. I forgot a step, hit the living room floor on the run.... WHACK !

The object was soft and spongy. "OW!" It also spoke. I couldn't make out the first sound, but the second was definitely human. Light flooded the room. More bodies, more noises. I had crashed straight into a sleepy teenage convention. Apparently the light snow of early evening had turned ugly and they couldn't get back to Mary's Harbour, so Margaret took them in. They all knew each other. The party included four; two Rumbolts, one Dyson, one Pye and now one ageing Howgate. I even recognized two. They'd just completed a one hundred mile round trip to visit girlfriends in Red Bay. It was your normal Friday night. Love was in the air and the symptoms of hormonal imbalance bagged their eyes. It was too early to match limbs with bodies and too late to judge their life signs. I made my apologies, turned the light switch off and left them to their dreams.

It took little persuasion next day to keep me in bed. My stomach was still bloated and rigormortis locked my joints. I did make a lame attempt to rise. Call it guilt, but one look at the horizontal snow pellets was enough to keep the sheets on. When I finally got up the day was half over, or so I thought. While I was asleep, Margaret had put together a social calender of events. Her parents expected me for supper, then a queue of other family members required my presence. There were no rigid time tables. If I didn't see them today, there was always tomorrow. They were all open-ended, "It would be nice to see you, but". For me there were no buts. Far from feeling obligated, I couldn't wait to see them all.

"Where do you come from?" "Are your parents still alive?" "What do you do for a living?" Marriage, children, the A to Z of life. They all asked for the story behind the story. I was probed, pushed and teased into submission. It was no good wearing a front, they were going to defeat me sooner or later. I thought it better to tell them all and hope for the best. As soon as they had built up a picture I was let off the hook and sent on to the next meeting.

By the third house my appetite had been stretched to the limit. "Have another cup-a-tea boy." "Finish off the pot or dog a'l have it." "Try just one more muffin." Try this, try that. I was among kindred spirits and my elastic stomach was turning into my greatest social asset.

That night was notable not only for food but also for gifts. I came away from the Pyes with a pair of sealskin gloves and later that evening I could have accepted a pair of snow shoes, a hand-knitted toque and some Labrador socks. I found that to compliment someone on something was tantamount to asking for it. I was in virgin territory. A polite refusal was met with a more determined offer to accept. I was in a no-win situation, a reverse bidding that in the end left me in limbo.

Back at Margaret's another surprise awaited me.

Labrador Regional Development Committee, in the person of Sandra Pye, had come up trumps with more information on the route ahead. I could feel the trip coming together. The coastal settlements that only two weeks before had been a mystery were coming to life. That wasn't all she brought. I found I was to be passed on down the trail. In Mary's Harbour, Denley Rumbolt and his girlfriend Sheila would put me up and in Port Hope Simpson it would be the Sampsons. I was on my way.

I could have stayed an extra day. The snow was blowing like the devil and the morning forecast was of more of the same. I was glad of it. To cover the six miles to Mary's Harbour in good weather would be too easy, but in dirty weather I would arrive with an appetite. My plan was to follow Lodge Bay's horse shoe harbour, cross the bridge, go to the top of the hill, then leave the road for the ski-doo trail. Easier said than done. The trail wound every which way but straight, and then there was snow, fresh snow, fresh deep snow. I got the workout I wanted and then some. It took me four hours to cover the distance and by the time I got there I was tired, hungry and damp.

Mary's Harbour can be summed up in one word, 'BAKEAPPLES'. I left Toronto a lean, mean 136 pounds. For three months prior to my departure I'd eaten like crazy, even worked out in a gym, all in the name of weight. I shouldn't have bothered. I'd already gained two pounds since arriving in Labrador and in Mary's Harbour I would double it.

Bakeapples are not so much a unique taste as a journey. Picked locally, their golden suntans set them apart. Some Newfies call them liquid gold and if given the choice would gladly adopt them as local currency. Whether cooked or eaten raw, it's impossible to take away their crunch. It's the pip that catches between the teeth that makes them special and the combination of bitter and sweet sent my taste buds crazy and turned me into an instant bakeapple junky.

I ate bakeapple jam for breakfast, bakeapple pie for dinner and crunchy baked apple squares for supper. I couldn't get enough and before leaving the Rumbolts, I crashed the 140 pound barrier.

Chapter 5
Toronto Man Drowns in Two Feet of Water

I HAD A STRONG FEELING I HAD TRAVELLED down this route before and the further I walked down Lewis Inlet the more certain it became. I was in a full-blown storm. Two hours before, I was having breakfast in Mary's Harbour. Outside the signs were bad; horizontal smoke, milk grey skies and a halo of haze where the sun should have been. There was no check-out time at the Rumbolts. I'd already stayed four nights and one more wouldn't be questioned. In all honesty it didn't look all that bad in the community, but on the exposed, ice-topped St. Lewis Inlet, the surface was smoking.

At first the young fern tree markers locating the trail down the Inlet were clearly visible. Set at one hundred feet intervals in the ice, I could make out over twenty, then it was down to ten. I hoped to take a break at Hatters Point before crossing to the north side of the Lewis river, but I kissed that idea goodbye when the markers started to jump out like sentries. I was in bad ice country. Visibility was non-existent and a decision taken to leave the trail now could easily end up being my last. There was nothing for it but to keep to the markers, find a walking rhythm and stick to it. Once again, easier said than done. The wind screamed at full throttle down the Inlet and the air was alive with snow. Underfoot was like walking in loose sand and pulling my sledge over its drifts like dragging a dead weight over dunes. At some point I turned around. My nose was chapped to the bone and I didn't fancy loosing it.

BANG! CRASH! WALLOP!

I was up and down like a yo-yo. It's hard enough

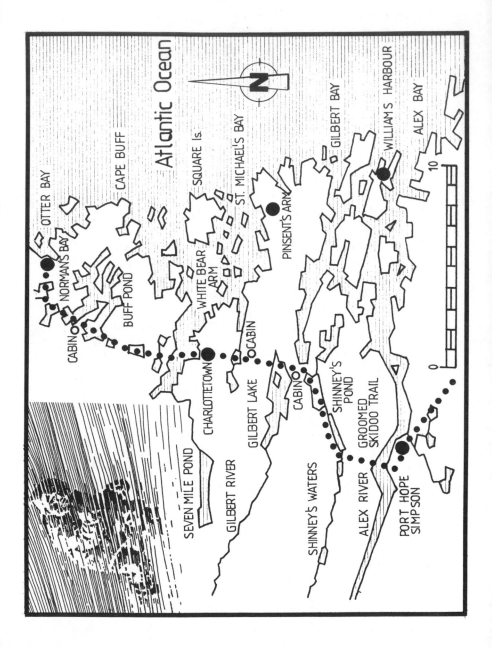

to find good footing bent over like a hunchback facing into the wind, but near impossible when walking blindly into it backwards.

By noon the wind had dropped and the snow had settled. The picture postcard scene returned and the Lewis showed me her better side. I could trace my steps back to Mary's Harbour and ahead a tapered V of white shaved off into a rolling sea of trees. I was now travelling on the north side some two hundred yards from shore. I was looking for a green cabin in which Denley had gone out earlier to light a fire. My plan had been to spend a night of cabin comfort, then strike out before dawn for Port Hope Simpson. I wanted to cover the distance in two days. That was the plan, but it didn't turn out that way.

I found the cabin easily enough. The fire was still lit and the pork chops, as promised, were bagged, thawed and hanging from the rafters ready to fry. The cabin had all the comforts of home; easy chairs, mattress, radio and even battery operated lights. The cabin's owner heard of my planned route, offered it for the night and left the keys with Denley.   My first unseen benefactor, but not the last; before the trip was over they would become a regular occurrence.

Life is not always a Walt Disney Picture. It's hard to enjoy the scenery when the windchill is minus 70 deg.C. and your lungs are bursting. To say it was a raw morning was an understatement. Cold, I am told, is just a matter, of comparison, while discomfort is just proof of one's bad adaptability. Those words were of little comfort. It was minus 36 deg.C. in the shade. The air was as bubbly as champagne and the sun troubled me even with my shades on. It took a good hour to get the blood circulating, then just when it reached the comfort level a call to nature started the whole process again. When I finally branched off the Lewis into the cut ski-doo trail, I exchanged the frigid cold and wind-hardened surface for the sheltered temperate zone of powdered snow. The trail groomer would have just left Fox Harbour that morning, and would have all on to reach Mary's Harbour by lunchtime, I would have to break trail until it passed or wait till a ski-doo laid down a track to follow. All afternoon I climbed. The fresh snow was still spongy and it was slow progress. I managed well enough over the ponds, and the wind-hardened crests were done in overdrive, but trouble always waited in the narrow wood cuts. Here the trail wound in and out of the trees and the slightest touch showered me with fresh powdered snow. I was crossing over a range of hills between Lewis Inlet and Alex River. Every crest opened onto unobstructed horizons of rolling hills, frozen rivers and overhanging curtains of healthy forest. In the last hour the sky had turned from arctic blue to gold to rusty brown. It was late afternoon and still no cabin. The groomer had passed long ago and I was going hell for leather. I was caught between risk and caution. I didn't relish the idea of putting up my tent on an exposed ridge, but I didn't want to risk finding my way to a cabin that could be further away than daylight. In the end I didn't have to choose. Two ski-dooers stopped for a chat and twenty minutes later I was sharing their fire. In two days I had covered 25 miles. I hadn't made Port Hope Simpson, but I did get to spend another night under roof. Tomorrow would be all down hill. I should be at the Sampsons by lunchtime.

There are some things better left for outsiders to find and bad ice is one of them. I had been warned about springs, tickles of strong current and seal holes, but I never thought a bust pipe would be one of them. One moment I was walking on firm ice, the next breaking through it. There was no sudden fall, more a slow motion dive. I wasn't even frightened; the only thought passing through my mind was one of embarrassment. Who but a fool could freeze to death in the middle of Port Hope Simpson? Imagine the headlines, "TORONTO MAN DROWNS IN TWO

FEET OF WATER'. I had no matches, no change of clothes, but luckily I was only a five minute walk from the Alex Hotel.

"Been for a swim, boy?"

What a sight I made. Ice from waist to foot. At minus 30 deg.C., clothes freeze-dried instantly. I was a hit with the patrons. Coffee and sandwiches appeared and my clothes hung up to dry in the boiler room.

What does a man in this place do to be noticed? Yesterday Port Hope Simpson was a ghost town. It's not that I had expected a ticker-tape welcome, but it would have been nice. Maybe it was my detergent that kept people away. I would like to think it was the windchill, but the truth was, my arrival clashed with that of 'ALL OUR CHILDREN'. It was soap time, the weekly religion and all eyes were glued to the box. It was just another day in the life of Adam, who was having if off with Gloria, who was in love with Stuart, who had eyes for Dixie. I didn't stand a chance.

That was yesterday, but today Bernie was the lead player. It was I who was down to my 'Calvin Kleins', but unlike television, I had no takers. Two complementary drinks later my clothes were dry, but as soon as I'd left the hotel I was tackled from behind.

I couldn't believe my eyes. The last thing I expected was to be felled by a grade four child sat astride a sled pulled by a puppy dog. I had heard of dog teams, but I thought that was just a rumour, a sales pitch directed towards tourism, but now I knew better. True, they'd been relegated to hobby status, but traditions die slowly in the north and just like their southern neighbors with horse racing, no winter sports day in Labrador is complete without its dog race.

Dogs started to disappear as soon as reliable snowmobiles were introduced in the late sixties. The decision was a practical one. A dog team is a living machine that you can't just turn off or even casually park with the motor running. When you park your snowmobile in spring, you don't have to feed it until the next winter. It's no coincidence that dogsled racing became a coastal sport within a decade after dog-mushing for transportation vanished.

I'm not overly enthusiastic about dogs. I was offered one in Red Bay, but I don't like dog meat. "They need too much attention", I said. They call as soon as the sun rises and are like five year old children who never grow up. Having said that, the dogs I'd seen so far on the coast were unlike any I had seen before. For starters they have that wiry look, and have more than a hint of wolf in their dark piercing eyes. They are like coils under pressure ready to pounce - not exactly your average cuddly poodle. You see them chained to stakes and circled by perfect 360 degree borders of faeces-stained, hard-packed snow. I had passed a group of three the other day. The first almost decapitated itself with excitement, the second didn't even stir, but the last, tail wagging like a helicopter stuck its nose between my legs and almost put an end to my sex life. I'm not an expert in the field of mushing, but after two weeks in the harness, I would say these dogs have the perfect bodies for pulling a sled; they all have broad chests, straight short backs and bushy tails, but most important of all, they have four legs and a passion for going forward.

My own dog team ! It sounded idyllic. I could sit on the komatik and enjoy the scenery with only the patter of paws and heavy breathing to share it with. After all, they could carry their own food, I was told. I almost gave in to the idea. I even enquired about availability and price, but when the night's orchestra of off-key howls hit the airways, I put all thoughts of dogs on the back burner.

Chapter 6
Winter Sports Day

THE OUTSIDE CLOCK READ MINUS 32 DEG.C There was zero wind and the sky was crystal clear. I left the Sampsons just as the sun's rays clipped the top of 'Blow-me-Down'. The open tickle on the Alex River was steaming and there was just a hint of salt in the air. Yesterday the trail groomer had ploughed its way past en route to Charlottetown. It was rock hard underfoot, ideal walking conditions. I had now been in Labrador three weeks, spent eight days walking on the trail and covered 100 miles. In that time the landscape had changed dramatically. The section from Red Bay to Mary's Harbour had been dominated by bald hills, then it was the broad frozen water of St. Lewis Inlet. All this time the trail gradually turned inland. Port Hope Simpson was five miles from the open ocean. Trees which had been non- existent on the Barrens took purchase of the land and the further I travelled the thicker and higher they grew. Even the sun was climbing higher. In the morning, sunlight shattered into a thousand rays. The trail's dark tunnel was streaked in lines of white and for one hour I walked on an endless shadow of railway track. By mid-morning the lines had shrunk. The sun floated above the trees and the trail returned to whiter than white. Strange things happened at noon; the surface would shimmer. Heat in February is imaginary, the sun's no more than an angry eye, but the illusion is enough to raise anyones spirits.

The groomed trail now cut deep into the wood and my horizons were only as far as the next bend. Yesterday had been a rare respite from the usual up and down of travel, but that was yesterday. Today a quick glance at the coastal route ahead was nothing less than intimidating. The trail north looked like a

fireman's step ladder of bisecting bays, inlets, and
rivers. Each waterway would have cut its own corre-
sponding deep valley.They would be no easy detours,
no bridges to smooth out the contours and it was only
going to get worse.

I was now passing through the most populated
section of the coast. There's only 50 miles separating
Mary's Harbour from Charlottetown. I was never
alone for long and this posed an unanticipated problem. The groomer tracked two narrow lanes, one
coming and one going. There was no room for error,
no passing lanes. The sound of a ski-doo pushed
alarm bells and the sight of them made me detour
instantly. There was always the possibility of being
hit. Blind bends were taken at speed and God help
me if I came face to face with a ski-doo when the bend
was combined with a steep gradient. Twice I had to
execute emergency exits and both times sunk up to
my armpits.

Ski-doo groups came in all sizes and from as many
directions. There were the young cruisers, the town
hoppers and the wood-cutters. They came singly, in
pairs and in large tribal groups bundled up to their
eyelids. They broke up my days, brought invitations
to spend the night or at the very least, "Do you want
a ride?" I remember vividly being stopped by a family out from Cartwright. I was the tonic they'd
prayed for and no sooner had they stopped when
their komatik bust into life. Two dog pups jumped
out, closely followed by three human ones. Michael
Jackson would have been hard pressed to get such
reactions and while their parents captured my every
gesture on video, their children rattled off questions
with the speed of a gattling gun.

I had been introduced to the ski-doo by a National
Geographic series on arctic lifestyles. On the square
screen they looked like a space odyssey version of
mutant ants on skate boards and if I closed my eyes I
could swear they sounded like killer bees. So far I'd
seen Arctic Cats, Polaris, Yamahas and the old faith-

ful Ski-doo. As yet they all looked the same, but I was getting there.

It was stop and start all day. Photo shoots and interviews, but still no cabin. I was starting to get worried. The sun was sliding rapidly and there was more shadow than light. At first I took the opening in front for a small pond, then as I got closer, a huge snow drift. It wasn't until I was on top of the cabin and saw its two black eyed windows and open door that I knew I had arrived.

I was soon stripped, changed and roasting, then just as I entered dreamland........BANG!!! The cabin flooded with light.

"Eh boy, how's it going?"

I jumped out of my dream, struck the shelf with my head and just missed impaling myself on a ski pole. "Sorry, did we wake you?"

There were four pair of eyes blinking in my direction. Three sticks and a doe boy. What a mixture. After the first exchange the bottom fell out of our conversation. I was all talked out after a long day. There were long pauses. My audience was putting a human face to the rumors about the 'Walking Man'. You can't shut the door of human contact in a ski-doo trail emergency shelter for long and now it had become the local drop-in centre. The group was from Charlotteown. They'd been out cruising, seen my sled propped up against the door and walked straight in.

"Are you stopping at Charlottetown?" The question was loosely wrapped around an invitation. "Yes." That's all it took and before they left I had been invited to stay with the Stone Family.

I was greeted to a spectacular morning. The sky was awash in bronze, and ferns, heavily weighed down from last night's snowfall, were coated as if dipped in its colour. I couldn't resist the opportunity to eat outside. It was minus 10 deg.C. but felt much warmer. I reheated last night's left-overs, demolished

two chocolate bars and drained six cups of coffee.
Food is a precious commodity in the bush and my
appetite didn't go unnoticed. Two grey jays worked
me over in tandem. I couldn't believe how cheeky
they were. Unlike their pork-bellied neighbors, the
ptarmigan and grouse, they are not exactly edible. I'd
heard they were the bushman's mascot. Obviously
this pair had staked out the cabin as their territory

and expected to be fed on a shared occupancy basis.
Within no time I had them eating out of my hand.
Then it was the turn of a robin, more jays and even a
squirrel got into the act. Suddenly a distinctive ariel
bark cleared the table. Coloured jet black like wet
coal, and with a transporter's wing span, a crow had
dropped in for a visit and was now perched atop a
tree and weighing up the situation. I can put up with
jays, look over the occasional chewed out hole in
equipment caused by squirrels, but crows and ravens
are big time nuisances. If it's not tied, nailed or

weighed down, then its open season. It doesn't have
to be edible. Some work on a barter system. A
colourful mitt is worth two slices of bread, a hat, a
chocolate bar and God help you if they take a liking
to your unguarded wallet.

I do believe they are more intelligent than wolves.
They don't go for the frontal assault; they like decoys,
smoke screens and mind games. In Port Hope
Simpson, I watched two crows work over a dog. He
didn't stand a chance. Within minutes they'd teased
the poor creature into a rabid frenzy. He was dive-
bombed, mugged and laughed at. Then when they
knew he was a crazed coil of power, they went on the
offensive. One crow perched itself on a metal bin,
waited for the certain pounce and timed it to perfection. The dog struck for thin air, hit the bin, knocked
it over and spewed out its contents. Game over. The
dog slunk away. A respectful time was allowed to
elapse, then it was on to the business of scavenging
garbage. Why dirty your hands for a living when you
can get others to do it for you? That's their motto, so
it was with this thought in mind that I decided to
pack up before a squadron of like-minded scavengers
appeared.

By the time I got started the wind had changed.
Above, the clouds were sullen. The light was shutting
down and every time the trees opened the trail melted into a frosty grey haze of snow and sky. My first
obstacle was a pond at the bottom of Gilbert Bay.
Here the trail entered a rusty patch of stained snow.
Bad ice? With an axe, I could have chopped down a
good stick for testing purposes in no time, but I did-
n't have one. It was no good crying over spilt milk. I
would have to go around it, but where? Last night's
snow had not yet settled. The ski-doo trail was covered, and to compound the situation, I couldn't see
any tree markers in the ice ahead. Could this be the
wrong trail? Everything pointed to the other side.
My map showed it and local information made it certain. The stain had spread while I thought. Could the

pond be tidal? That fact was on another map, not the one I had. The stain seemed to start from the brook and spread outwards. I discounted a tide, guessed on running water, hoped that the clean patch of ice I was heading for wasn't a section hung up on rocks and went for it.

I spent the next sixty minutes breaking trail over dubious overhangs of fresh snow, through thick bush and tiptoeing over suspect ice. The snow was so powdery that even with my snow shoes I sunk up to my knees and on more than one occasion the sled flipped. I was now away from the stained ice and out of trouble. A likely story! The sound of a crack, followed by surface movement downwards, turned my hair grey. I was still harnessed to my sled. I had visions of eternal anchorment underwater to my equipment. Needless to say, I didn't hang around and once the point ahead was rounded, tree markers appeared on the pond. I was back on track.

Once I was across it, the trail took off almost vertically. It was calorie burn-up time again and for the next thirty minutes I struggled from tree to tree, bush to bush, branch to twig, until I reached the top exhausted. I was now too tired to descend using the more traditional methods of rope brakes, so throwing caution to the wind, I lay back on my equipment, crossed my fingers and let the sled take charge.

I didn't see my first ski-doo until I'd passed Pinsent's Arm turn-off. By now it was snowing, not heavily, but just enough to keep the temperature up and make the surface sticky. The short sharp hills made me sweat and what breeze there was lost itself to the surrounding trees. It was like being in a turkish bath. Then suddenly the trail opened. The air moved. A mild breeze quickly turned into a stiff wind and by the time it closed again the windchill froze all my sweat.

My arrival in the settlements always made me nervous. I felt that all eyes were on me, like an

entrance on stage. It wasn't ego or conceit, it was
worry. Would I find a place for the night? Had my
name been passed down the trail as promised? Would
he or she remember me. I shouldn't have worried. I
was expected. Patsy Stone had prepared a meal of
piping hot caribou stew and, having given it full jus-
tice, Bernie collapsed in a heap in front of the television.

All this time, life in Labrador went on as normal.
School had finished, young and old popped in to the
Stone household, stayed, ate and then left. I lost track
of who was who. Faces and names overlapped by the
hour. No one seemed to be into head counts. There
were the inevitable telephone calls, a raised voice
down the phone, a plea, then one less. That night I
slept in the basement. A couch, a leg, a twisted body.
I was now used to it, the questions ,did I take a family bed or was it for a visitor? remained unasked. I
now put it down to friendly confusion, slipped
between some empty sheets and left it at that.

In the morning the basement was empty. A clean
sweep of overnighters.That was the way. People came
and went; relatives, boyfriends and girlfriends and
visitors like myself. The welcome mat of hospitality
had a permanence that read welcome anytime, anywhere, and I was slowly becoming accustomed to it.

On the second day, I went for a walkabout. I was
here for the dog races, so that's what I was looking
for. Some liken a penned-up husky team to a state of
continual warfare. Well, when I saw my first, I could-
n't make out who was making the most noise, the
dogs or the children. Mind you, it was hard to tell the
difference. They who grow up together, fight together and lie together will invariable pick up on each
others characteristics and there isn't much difference
between a dog and a child when they're underfoot.

That evening Charlottetown's doggy ensemble
outdid themselves. For the uninitiated like myself, a
dog's bark as a deterrent comes a close second to the

sight of its teeth. A husky dog is not so gifted When the Almighty was handing out the voice boxes he must have overlooked the breed.   They just can't bark; try as they might, they will always remain in limbo, somewhere between falsetto and soprano, but its doggy loss is a human gain. There is nothing like a team of dogs in an operatic mood. Howling, I was told, could be started by such diverse things as the sound of a church bell, hunger, hormonal imbalance or just plain boredom. A single individual picks the first note and holds it until all his neighbors within earshot have agreed, then together like an orchestra they switch to a higher note. This lasts but for a few moments. Group unison always falters, howls stutter, take off on tangents and a few, plain out of puff, stop completely, only to start again upward through the scales. These overlapping notes go on for a while then join once more for a last dying note before cutting off into a sharp silence. Whew! Love, em or hate, em, the sound haunts you and unlike cats it's no good throwing an old boot at them unless you want it tenderized.

At the first sound of a plane I took off to the store. It was the mail winging in on Lab Air from St. Anthony, Nfld. I was thirsty for gossip. With the exception of my food parcels, I'd not heard from anyone since Toronto. Any news would be good news; Dear John's, bills, even a Simpson Sear's catalogue would be read from cover to cover. I didn't care what it was or from whom it came. I'm not usually a great letter writer. It's hard to manufacture interest out of everyday life, but here things were new, every corner begged investigation.   I was bursting with stories, and my pen had never been as active. In the last three weeks I must have fired off twenty letters, written 5000 words, and stretched every new adventure to the limit. Now I was all played out.

I hadn't expected mail in Red Bay. In Mary's Harbour it would have been a bonus, but to receive nothing in Port Hope Simpson was demoralizing.

The post office had been my first port of call on reaching a community. "Any mail for Bernie Howgate?" "Sorry, nobody loves you."

My mind needed to escape, touch base with friends and know that they cared. I was beginning to understand why the fantasy love novels, the revolving door of visitors and the art of conversation were still alive and well on the coast. They were all whiffs of life before the tube. Three weeks ago I could have switched moods as easily as T.V. channels; all I needed was my remote. Now I was suffering from withdrawal.

Waiting in the store was like judgement day. I'd never given letters much thought before, but now I realized their importance. The place was packed to overflowing. It seemed the mail was not the only excuse to meet and gossip. I was told fresh fruit and veggies were on their way. Weeks of spotty bananas, spongy apples and limp cabbage would drive anyone into queue. Apparently it's common practice for the community stores to fly in their perishables. Everything else comes in by boat. The last one to make it before freeze-up was in November and the next wouldn't be expected before June. Eight months between boats, you'd better believe space was at a premium. What you saw was what you got. Shelves floor to ceiling and a window display of storage. Expiry dates were meaningless, everyone knew when they came. There were open boxes of chips, Pepsi and Diet Coke. The usual tinned goods and essential hardware were there, but the cleanest section, the areas that had been worn down from greatest use, had the labels flour, yeast, baking powder, condensed milk and tinned Vienna sausages. These were downright necessities, and God forbid that the store proprietor run out of tobacco.

"Bernie , your mail" I came out smelling of roses. I was in love, well not quite, but she hadn't forgotten me.

Back at the ranch, Earl Stone was getting stuck

into his caribou. My arrival had coincided with his return from Churchill. Every year he hunted the George River Caribou Herd and this year had been no different. Caribou meat took care of 25% of his family's protein and it would be a bad year if he didn't fulfill his family's licensed quota. Each adult on the coast is allowed two caribou and when you take into consideration the time it takes to ski-doo from Charlottetown to Churchill, the temperatures you travel in minus 40 deg. C and the price of gas for the 1100 mile round trip, you don't do it for sport. For him, shooting caribou was no different than you or I going to the meat market. At the moment his work shed was a butcher's block of meat, hair and skin. The animals had taken two days to thaw and now I was sitting back, watching the carver in him cut and hacksaw joints of meat ready for the freezer. It was as natural to him as that of an abattoir worker, but when his uncle appeared to take his caribou away and proceeded to tie one end of the rope around its back legs and the other to the back of his ski-doo, I knew the sight of a dead frozen caribou bouncing around in the snow would be too much for the delicate city palate of most of my friends.

Picture a fan of lines under tension, add to it a noise resembling the squeals of pre-school excitement, then give it a shake just for the the hell of it. What you get is a harness dog team gone crazy. Huskies aren't exactly thoroughbred prima donnas, but they certainly don't suffer from being overly patient. I don't know which is more exciting, their pre-race antics, the start or the finish. Today the prize money would be secondary to bragging rights. The make-up of competitors had all the ingredients of a local Derby. William's Harbour, Pinsent's Arm, St. Lewis, Port Hope Simpson. Each community was in spitting distance from the other and rivalries ran deep. It was the stuff of romance. The colours were brighter than bright, the vocals heated and the smell of dogs punched the air. I'd waited 5 days for the race and wanted to savour every last moment.

To the untrained eye the teams looked a tangled mess of traces. Dogs, handlers, spectators, everyone got in the act. There were last minute adjustments, jockeying for positions and the inevitable old scores bit into, then just as I thought the race would be abandoned.....BANG! They were off. Thirty traces, six tight fans.

"YEH BOY, I, I, I ,I, COO, COO, COO"

Twenty minutes later the crowd had dispersed. Sports day was in full swing. The shooting range had opened and I could hear thuds coming from the wood chop competition and loud burst of laughter from the tortuous rope somersault.

After thirty minutes the dog teams were smudges in the distance. I was still rooted, bitten by the bug, and by the circles of warmth in the snow, I was not the only one. It was brew-up time; a snow picnic of freshly brewed tea on open fires, Kraft sandwiches, Vienna sausages, crisps and Pepsi. Occasionally a ski-doo would drive by, give a race update, then it was back to the binoculars and a second cup of tea. After two hours the lead team had the crowd back. It was all over, bar the shouting. William's Harbour dog team was streets ahead. What a sight. You could make out puffs of steam. Tails lopped like dislocated rudders and tongues trailed in the snow. The driver was ruddy red and frost stuck to his whiskers like icicles. He was full of himself and crossed the finish line like a veteran showman, flipping over the komatik and bringing the whole scene to a full stop. The pause was only momentary; dog race etiquette dictated a three lift aerial throw on his komatik and while his supporter chaired him, children tripped, petted and bathed the dogs in snow. That wasn't the end; the sports day continued till dark. Then it was onto the community centre. A Pot Luck Supper, prizes and then a dance.

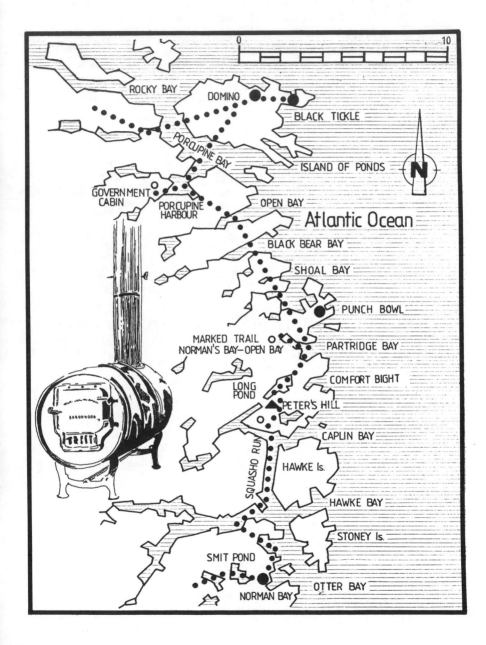

Chapter 7
A Faded Line of Information

IWAS SEDUCED BY A SILVERY MOON. OUTSIDE the path was cast in diamonds. It was that time of day and I'd just got the calling. What an idiot. I had visions of freezing to death with my trousers down. I could have done it in the outhouse, but no, Bernie wanted to do it in the great outdoors. I'm no stranger to toilets. On this trip my bottom had been pampered, splintered and suffered from the occasional chap. I've sat on everything from soft foam, wood chip to the 'honey bucket' of squatters rights and you can even put forward the argument that you haven't lived until you have experienced the sight of a stalagmite formation of frozen faeces! I always lit a candle before leaving camp, it was my life line. I'd look back, see the yellow streak of light and follow it, but what do you do when the light goes out and all you have on is your boots and your thermals. Think quick and act in reverse. By the time I got back to the cabin I was frigid with cold.

I was now half way between Charlottetown and Norman's Bay. I left the Stone's at the crack of dawn. I made excellent progress on a freshly groomed trail and reached Cape Buff Cabin by sunset. Once again, people stopped, offered rides and, as before, made my arrival at cabins a warm one. My earlier fears of the unknown were behind me. I was becoming familiar with the country, its moods,and its people. I wasn't treated like an intruder anymore, the city boy strutting his stuff, but as a kindred spirit. Maybe this was because I was walking, or maybe it was because I took people as they took me - with a pinch of salt and a little humour.

Until Mary's Harbour, Norman's Bay had been a mystery. My map called it Lady's Arm. It wasn't even a dot. I originally took it for a summer fishing community, deserted in winter, now I was about to be swallowed by its sleepy generosity. After days of scentless travel communities were always announced by the sweet smell of burning wood and, once I was spotted, by a chorus of its barking dogs. The first thing that struck me on the coast were the homes. They were all wood. Most were box-like, four convnient corners and a roof, but here and there the odd one still retained that add-on look and a few more had the picture postcard window and door moldings painted in vivid red and green. Central heating and microwaves were the norm, no different from a city family with its one point two children. That was on the surface, but you only had to see past their nintendo games to find the east coasts flip side. Norman's Bay community of eleven families was a prime example.

To cross their thresholds was like entering a time machine. The first door opened into a storage area of wood and hardware called the porch. You were now one step away from the inner cloister, because the next door opened into the kitchen. Here I found wood burning cast iron stoves still in use for heating and cooking, black and white televisions constantly crackled and clothes hung as they fell on the floor. Every room had that lived-in look, where you could just as easily see a ski-doo engine stripped for repair on the kitchen floor as baking on its table. Life in these communities continues going forward but with one eye on the rear view mirror. Isolation helps this view and blood lines cement it.

Blood ties on the Labrador coast run deep. In Lodge Bay nearly all the surnames were Pye. In Mary's Harbour every other one was a Rumbolt and in Port Hope Simpson the Pennys ran everything from the post office-cum-store to the Alexis Hotel. In Charlottetown the Campbells and Turnbulls were evenly matched and here in Norman's Bay all except two were Wards.

I was now definitely in tea country; invitations were sealed with it. Tea wasn't just a tradition, it was a religion, and God forbid you ask for the herbal variety. Water was always on the boil and it wouldn't be long before the kitchen table was full of oven-fresh bread and homemade jams. The next ritual would take me into the living room. Here I would receive a lesson in genealogy as family histories were recorded in picture frames from B & W to colour, and it didn't take a family planning expert to work out that the old fashioned bed had more uses than for sleep.

Norman's Bay is one of those isolated outposts that cable T.V. forgot about and that Bell Canada is just getting to. They still have no wharf, no indoor plumbing and the brook is the only reliable source of water. That's one side of the equation. The other has no fences, an abundant wilderness and a quality of life that can only be judged if you can swim in many cultures.

My arrival there coincided with a change in weather. A strong easterly and ice pellets. Last night's cold fright had reduced my resistance and now I was suffering. The coastal dampness searched out old injuries - dislocated collar bone, leg fractures and a broken arm. I didn't need an x-ray as a reminder, I just knew. On top of this I was worried about tomorrow. The trail ahead was a faded line of information. It was patchy at best, and with no groomed trail to follow and few to no markers, I would have to rely on map and compass readings. The uncertainty of not knowing the right trail to follow scared me. On the barren coastal hills and bays the trails were not always visible. I followed the path of least resistance, but old wood cuts, forks in the trail and hunting parties going nowhere in particular had wrong-footed me on more than one occasion. I could afford it then, I had escape routes, community proximity and the certainty of ski-doos, but not this time.

Cartwright was over 60 miles away. You only travel that distance if you have to. There were no escape routes, just two private cabins at Partridge Bay and Porcupine Bay, and the settlement of Black Tickle was still a maybe. The only habitation was in Punch Bowl, a government wharf and fishplant that was manned by a winter maintenance crew of one. But that was miles off the trail. If that wasn't enough I was now entering Polar Bear country. The only polar bear I'd ever seen was in a book and that was how I wanted to keep it. The only good to come out of the day was meeting Philip Snow, the school's principal. I was all wiped-out, my head felt like a bag of beans and my nerves were shot. His wife rustled up a meal, changed the sheets, and I'd no sooner polished off the last crumb when I was history.

The worst scenario happened. Snow and lots of it. I could have excused myself from leaving if the sky had held more, or if strong winds were called for, but no such luck. I wanted to roll over, close my eyes and change the skies. Yesterday ten hunters passed en route to Churchill via Cartwright. I had built my hopes on their fresh trail. Now it was gone and I had no idea when the next ski-doo would pass.

It wasn't all beyond me. Local knowledge, slow in coming, now covered three pages. The key, I was told, was in the conditions. Fresh snow could open a tickle of thin ice overnight and a strong easterly turn sea ice into slob just as quickly. Caution in this section would be the rule rather than the exception. Yesterday's hunters had a guide with them and more than one person in Norman's Bay had offered to break trail to Porcupine Bay, but I had to strike out on my own sometime, and there was no time like the present.

Walking in snow shoes is an art form. Trial and error had been my excercize book. The technique of throwing one foot in front of the other, swivelling my hips and using arms for balance worked well on the flat, but on steeper gradients my knees buckled and I was left at the mercy of improvisation.

I knew that the locals took chances over ice, but

they knew the conditions. A ski-doo under full throttle can skip over bad ice, hydroplane over short distances of open water and power across bays in a fraction of the time it took by foot. We travelled under different rules. Controlled speed was their saving grace. I always planned two steps ahead, working on the principle that it's much easier to fall through ice than to get out of it, and going by the numerous large craters of sunken snow ahead, caution didn't lend itself to short cuts. I stayed away from banks of rocks and took to portaging over necks of land, wind-hardened bay ice, fresh water, ponds and barren ground. Among the soft trails I often got stuck. It made me want to give up and sit down, but that didn't help. Even in sheltered areas, frostbite was only moments away. I found the best way to get through these periods was controlled anger. I'd curse my way to tops of snow banks and stuck my chin out at the wind. Not exactly one with nature, but it worked and most of all it kept me warm.

By noon I'd left the wooded areas and ponds behind and was travelling over sea ice down Squasho Run. To the east, Hawke Island was half a mile away and to the west the mainland dropped vertically in cliffs of rock. It was a bleak place. Deep, open and windy and when it started to snow, dark shapes took on an eerie look. By late afternoon my vision shut down and I was going by compass. It was impossible to stop. The mainland was a wall of rock. To let go of it now and cross over to Hawke Island's sheltered shoreline looked the worse of two evils. When the snow eventually stopped, I found myself at a junction between Caplin Bay, Hawke Island and the open sea. Exposed wasn't the word for it. I felt naked. So much open ice! I scanned the north shore with my binoculars. I was looking for a tongue of snow between trees, the brook path to Peter's Hill. I was aiming for an old trappers' tilt (one room shelter). It's not that I wanted to sleep there. That wasn't important. What I was looking for was clear evidence that I was on the right trail. I didn't have to worry long. I spotted two lights coming in my direction and ten minutes later I had all the answers. It was Doug Kippenhuk. He'd left Punch Bowl that morning and filled me in with latest conditions. By evening I was at the tilt. The door was broken, snow had drifted and it was packed from floor to ceiling. Tonight would be my first night under canvas.

Tent errrection starts with a solid foundation. The first job was to pack down the snow and layer it with boughs (branches of fern trees). I then emptied the sled, layed out my tarp and spread the contents on it. After a hard day in the harness, I could wash my hands in snow if I wanted to and feel none the worse. It was like stepping out of a sauna into a cold shower. For a few minutes you felt nothing, then slowly you cooled down. Doing small things with my mitts on increased the time factor of tent erection by four, so when ever possible I exposed my hands to the cold using only my thin nylon gloves.

I had the tent poles slotted through their seams in no time and the fly sheet-cum-vestibule was up before my fingers went numb. It was then back to my mitts and phase two; interior decoration. I threw in my two duffel bags, opened my sleeping bag and put things in order, ready for dark. Torch, candle, radio and gun at one side, spare clothes and food on the other. Finished, I could now turn my energies to something I always looked forward to. Wood collection, great big pyramids of it, twice as much as I needed. A fire was a perfect centerpiece for all my thoughts, an end of day experience and worth all the day's efforts. The dark blanket of night, a silhouette of spruce, flickering stars and a roaring fire. I soon had a pot full of snow melted, then I fired up my white gas stove, boiled up a flask of tea and emptied a packet of dehydrated food into the remainder for the slow simmer on dying embers. With food on the boil and thirst quenched, I could set about readying myself for the night. First, I exchanged my boots for down filled slippers, brushed surface snow off clothes and swept the floor clean. I was ready for bed. I stripped down to thermals, stored socks, mitts and sweater in my sleeping bag. Ten minutes later I would be filling my belly and twenty minutes after that, I'd be in bed; heaven, or so it should have been.......

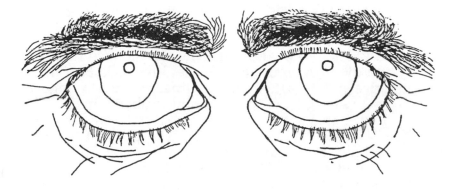

We all have hidden fears. They can be shared with loved ones, suppressed in crowds or blocked out through activity, but sometimes there is no escape. Fear can creep up like a thief in the night, strip you bare and leave you climbing walls. The clinical term is ' temporary insanity'. I've had my fair share over the years and no trip is complete without at least one visit to your soul.

Loneliness is always the main ingredient. I have always been seduced by that faraway place, the one that begs adventure. I still suffer from the child inside me. The awe of things new is a powerful force and that's why I was in Labrador, on my own.

Fear of the unknown is natural. It can be real or imaginary. I have never suffered from the real variety. If I can touch, taste or see it, I can cope. If it's abstract, I can't. My fears are elusive. They can be triggered by music, a shape in the water or a cloud in the sky. Tonight it started as a smell, then curved around the tent in the flickering shadow of candle light.

I'd not felt good all day. Food went untouched and now my mind was playing tricks. Hands buckled into arthritic shapes, skin burned, peeled, then melted like wax under heat. The tent closed in and I felt as trapped as a miner in a fall. It was awful. My legs were like rods of heated lead and my sleeping bag was being squeezed by the claustrophobic feeling of helplessness. I had to get out, out of the tent and to hell with the cold.

God knows how I did it. The stars looked friendly and the frost brought me back. I felt sick. Fear has its price and its taste lingered. I nearly stuck a finger down my throat, but the cold night sobered me.

I write this with a tinge of embarrassment. I'm no hero. I have an Achilles heel. Maybe it all meant something, but who cares? Maybe some Freudian student of travel will trace the dream back to my mother's milk. Maybe it stems from the day my dad dropped me on my head, or as one girlfriend warned me, 'it was God's punishment for thinking with my brain, but acting between my legs.' We all have our different ways of coping with low points. Some search for hidden meanings on the couch of psychiatry and others, like myself, laugh them off and move onto the next one as slowly as possible.

I awoke stuck to my sleeping bag. Hair fused to fabric and boots froze solid, as if on guard duty. Inside, the tent walls were coated in ice crystals and the slightest touch showered me. My gortex clothes froze as they lay in twisted folds and crunched like biscuits on my back. It was frigid even by February's standards, minus 34deg. C and it was still thirty minutes before sunrise. My whole body felt like the 'night after' and complained at every movement. The experience knocked me sideways. My first night under the stars and I'd turned into a whimp. What did I expect, air conditioning? In a cabin you could always stoke up the fire, crawl back to bed and wait for the thermometer to rise. In the tent my only rise came from a frustrated sex drive and even that was suspect. Fresh snow didn't help either. My sled was buried in a snow drift and my first steps left me ear to toe in its dusty shower. Breaking camp was an exercise in slow motion. It wasn't until I took an on-the-spot jog that my blood thinned and my old ticker spluttered to life.

It was fair pounding by the time I broke camp but one hour later a fuse blew. Peter's Hill, Peter's Bloody Mountain more like. I was standing at the foot of an almost vertical wall of snow. I had visions of altitude sickness, free fall and years in traction. Climbing the Eiger couldn't be worse. Choosing the best route up wasn't the problem, it was how to start it. Should I strip the sled and carry reduced loads or just go for it? I sunk my teeth into the latter and set off on a zig-zag course of upward motion.

Initial enthusiasm took me so far, but no further. My snow shoes were already history - too much strain. It was either my bindings or my skin and I needed both. I wasn't a quarter up before I was trailing my nose on all fours. My back was on fire. The only respite came from turning and shifting positions. I'd pull a little, change, drag a little, stop, rest, sprint, then collapse. Half way up the gradient eased. The ridge opened, swept in a slow arc and levelled off. It was a small victory. I found a couch of snow, took a pit stop, then went back at it again. I don't know how long it took or how many gallons of sweat I lost. All I remember is that I made it. From the top my trail looked like that of a drunken spider pulling a stick. I could see two scars in the snow where I flipped, the huge hole that buried me and the two beds I collapsed in. I could trace my trail all the way back to the tilt and the view down Squasho Run was amazing. I was dizzy with exhaustion, but I wanted to get over the top and away from the wind before resting.

What a wicked view. I couldn't believe my eyes. A window of sea, a silhouette of mountains, blue hazes and waves of green. Below I could make out the outline of a long pond, a treeless barren and the beginnings of Partridge Bay. The coast looked like the ragged edges of a book and due to the sea ice it was almost impossible to separate coastal islands from the mainland. At times like these, adrenalin rushes collide head on with fatigue and your body switches onto a different plane. It's a natural high; horizons stretch, lights flash and the mind explodes with colour. It was worth all the morning's pain and the experience lingered all the way past Comfort Bight and beyond.

I was now bursting with confidence. The scout inside me was in total control and my self-trained eye could spot clues like a eagle. Shredded caribou moss; stained snow; they were signs of mechanical travel.

The snow was beginning to settle and by the time I dropped down to Long Pond, shallow ski-doo tracks were clearly visible. The day was brilliant, my best yet.   Fiords, frozen bays and now deep lush healthy woods. Even the wind helped. It crusted the snow and made breaking trail as easy as walking on pavement.

At Partridge Bay I risked what looked like bad ice rather than follow the tree markers to Punch Bowl and away from my set course. It wasn't stupid, but all the same this development of set goals was a definite symptom of my solitude. Another was daydreaming.

When walking, your mind wanders like your feet. An old lover pops into your mind, twists, curls, then falls out of view. Sometimes an old song replays itself. For no particular reason during this trip I had adopted the Cowboy Junkies song '200 MORE MILES' as my theme tune. I often craved exotic foods and sometimes, to pacify myself, would play out a restaurant scene and struggle to recall every morsel. On more than one occasion I caught myself talking to shadows. If you daydream best in a soft armchair listening to classical music, Labrador isn't for you.

What a difference thirty minutes makes. When

you are on your own, you hold something back for safety's sake. Weather changes fast on the east coast and it's hard to relax and enjoy the views when survival is uppermost in your mind. Well, today I did and now the devil had returned for his payment. I'd no sooner rounded Crow's Head than it started to snow, huge heavy flakes of it. I knew I was less than two miles away from shelter. I was heading for a private cabin at the toe of Partridge Bay. It should have been less than sixty minutes away, yet it took me over two hours. Broken ice, crusty sea slob and drifting snow had me detouring all over the place and by the time I got there I was ravenous.

The highlight of the day was the evening meal; nothing was enough. Variety mattered little and I confess I tend to eat like a child, eating first what I like best and making a whole meal out of it. During the day I ate chocolate bars and in the evening whatever freeze-dried food popped into my hand. My fluid requirements were eight pints a day. I drank like a fish in the morning, stored it like a camel during the day, then topped it up again in the evening. Tonight there was an added bonus. Caribou meat, heaps of it, bagged and stored behind the porch door. I didn't look at it as stealing, just sharing. I just wanted a few slivers of meat to add taste to the evenings stew. Nothing more, nothing less. To understand my actions, you have to picture the cabin's location and know why it was there. It was built by people from Black Tickle and it acts as a base camp for hunts and wood collection. They were messages penned and pinned all over the place. Dates, times and mini-memos of information. There is an unwritten law for users. Replace wood and eat just enough, never all. They were common sense laws. People came and went all the time. Not many, but enough to make Neighborhood Watch a reality. Ski-doo tracks were like fingerprints and, as for me, I couldn't take a leak without someone down the trail knowing about it. Before turning in, I split a dozen logs, pinned up a message and left two bags of freeze-dried food for the next person.

When the sun shines even the barrens look inviting, but when the sun hides behind dark clouds, Labrador looks a desperate place. My nightly weather forecast had been lost to static. The first warning sign was the temperate, minus 5 deg C; the second was wind direction, south east; and the third was the morning halo round the sun. Florida was coming north and by mid-day I was stripped down to my thermals.

I made Black Bear Bay in double quick time, but there was a reason for haste. The weather was closing in fast. The sky was full of snow and it was only a matter of time. The route from Partridge Bay to Shoal Bay had been a piece of cake. Once I'd located the trail on the north shore opposite Crow's Head, it was just a lesson in drainage. You hop on a brook, step up a level, cross a pond, jump to the next, then follow its drainage system down. The ponds were as solid as rocks and gradients shallow, and with few trees to obscure the view I had ideal map and compass conditions. But the weather changed rapidly crossing Black Bear Bay. Clouds dropped and the sun shattered. 'White out' conditions. This time it caught me after I spotted the bright yellow ski-doo marker on its north shore, but no sooner had I passed the marker than it was swallowed in snow. It was1:00pm, too early to stop, but I would be pushing it to get over the barrens to Open Bay before nightfall. I took a break and weighed up the pros and cons. Black Bear Bay offered little protection; stunted trees, a few rocks and exposed bay ice. If I put up my tent now and the snow stopped I'd kick myself. Open Bay held the promise of ideal shelter. I knew the groomed trail to Cartwright and Black Tickle started there. I still had plenty of energy and today's compass readings had been spot on. I had learned the language of map reading and the barren ahead looked no different than the two previous ones I'd crossed that day. I sat down on my sled, finished my flask of coffee, ate a chocolate bar, then mulled over the decision with a cigarette.

Thank God, the days were getting longer. Two weeks ago I wouldn't have given myself a hope in hell of making it, but today was different. I didn't ease up once and only allowed myself the luxury of a rest when Open Bay came into view. It was 4:30pm, sixty minutes to get from A to B and only forty-five minutes before sunset.

I put the tent up in twilight, cooked under the moon and ate my supper under the stars. Icing on the cake....Oops, every time I get cocky something happens to spoil my digestion.

.........BLIZZARD.............

The leading edge of the blizzard rolled in on cue at 8:00pm. By 8:30pm my fire had died and by 9:00pm I was out of it. I stayed in that state until 11:00pm. Fine grains of snow were drifting, not outside but in. The wind was howling and searching out the tent's weak spots. Everything was covered in a fine film of snow. I was worried; dampness is a killer. If the snow got into my sleeping bag and melted, its down-fill would soak it up like a sponge. Insulation values would be halved. This thought knocked the sleep out of my eyes.

First I had to locate the pin holes in the tent wall and then bandaid them. My sleeping bag had to be turned inside out, beaten and then checked with my flash light. Next I turned my attention to the tent floor. Cleaning fine snow particles is an exercise in frustration; snow hides everywhere. The slightest brush had it floating to all corners. Needless to say, I was freezing when the job was finished and for the rest of the night I struggled with sleep.

I woke to find half my tent in deep shadow. It was buried in a huge drift. That was only the beginning of my problem. Thankfully the tent opened at both ends, so at least I didn't have to dig myself out, but I'd left the vestibule open all night and now it was plugged solid with snow.   Equipment had to be painstakingly sifted out, checked, then packed away. Locating my snow shoes was hopeless, and had it been a less important item, I would have left them buried.   One hour later I was counting the damage. Lost, one 1: 50,000 map encompassing Porcupine Bay to Black Tickle, my stove's reflective heat foil, my gas flask container's screw top and my neck warmer. It was 10:00 o'clock before I broke camp. The morning weather forecast still gave out blizzard warnings, yet the sky was crystal clear. It was the calm before the storm and I didn't want to hang around to enjoy the scenery before it struck. Today's plan was to head for the 'Government Cabin' down Porcupine Bay.   It shouldn't have been a problem, but now I was using a 1:250,00 scale map. There was no detail. My thumb covered the whole bay and by now I couldn't make out whether I was on a large pond, a broad river, or the bay itself. Then......... gunfire! What the hell?

Chapter 8
The Blizzard

IMAGINE A SPACE JAM-PACKED WITH BODies. In one corner we had the stove with its heat worshippers while in the other a table surrounded by excited card-thumping gamblers. No-mans land was filled with nicotine smog and everywhere there was the constant queue for attention. You guessed it, the sound of gun fire had led me right into the tail end of a 'Rangers' Convention. They had just completed a weekend of survival techniques, map and compass lessons and a shooting competition and now it was time to relax, count up the scores and celebrate with a six pack.

I fit straight into the mood like an old glove. Peas pudding, pork chops, fresh bread and a Molson, and by the looks of the large coleman coolers stored in a corner there was plenty more where that came from.

If there was one thing I'd learned about coastal ski-doo travel it was that people prepare for the worst and hope for the best. Even when travelling only short distances from one community to the next many will take tent, stove and enough food to last many days if snow-bound. Axe, spare clothes and camping gear are not just necessary but normal requirements and these rangers had them all in spades.

Like all amateur armies, these volunteer Rangers were all generals.Opinions overlapped, egos bumped and decibals went through the roof. Everyone seemed to understand that normal rules of conduct were suspended away from your better halves. Outrageous circumstances called for outrageous behavior and they weren't about to let the opportunity go unnoticed. It was not the atmosphere for the genteel of manner or nervous disposition. It was in fact your normal heavy duty male bonding where even a fly on the wall covered his ears. And when the old squeeze box came out it was time to bend the floor boards.

The Rangers came from all walks of life-fishermen, clerks, shopkeepers-and came from as far afield as the Straights in the south to Rigolet in the north. Their plan was to spend one more night in Porcupine Bay celebrating, then start out home in the morning. This decision was by no means unanimous. The contingent from Black Tickle had other things on their minds. Maybe they knew something we didn't. They had sat through supper in a sullen mood. Two had slipped away almost unnoticed, then within minutes two more had their guns, coolers and a few logs of wood packed away on their komatiks and were gone.

All through the evening the wind rose. Snow was now building up by the door and sudden gusts creaked the cabin like a wooden sailship. The temperature was noticeably dropping and open doors could be felt all through the room. By night-fall the comings and goings had stopped and the blizzard had arrived. Anyone who wasn't sleeping over in our cabin had left for their own. And what I saw is what I got, for it would be over twenty four hours before anyone would dare venture between cabins. The wind was now deafening, and to open the door risked losing it. Even the darkness was darker than usual and torch light went no further than the first few flakes.

If downstairs was cool, upstairs was a steam bath. Bedtime found me climbing over bodies who lay as they had talked. There was no order. You picked a spot and crashed out. I fell asleep as the cabin swayed. It was the rockiest quarters I ever slept in and on more than one occasion I woke to bumps in the night and the occasional shower of snow powder that had forced its way in through the roof void.

The next day was even worse. Records were being broken. C.B.C. radio news was full of hurricane force winds, power failures and evacuations. Apparently Black Tickle was taking it on the chin. We weren't much better. There wasn't a tree, branch or twig within stone's throw of our cabin. Exposed wasn't the right word and being ten miles away from Black Tickle, what they got, we had ditto.

I did venture out for a moment. Twenty paces, that's all, but they were nearly my last. I wanted to take a picture of the cabin, but I ended up focusing up against a white wall. It was the worst experience of my life. Ten feet either way and I would have been just another news item. I guess my inexperience and naivete stuck out all over. My face was a sheet of ice and my expression told its own story. A hot mug of tea calmed me down and the Ranger's broadside of jokes put it all into perspective.

By the third day we were down to wood chips. A scouting party was formed, left and returned two hours later like blocks of ice. I couldn't believe how they stood the cold. Foolish or brave, by their standards the experience didn't even rate a mention and they were genuinely embarrassed when I pressed the point. It wasn't the first time I'd experienced this offhand attitude towards extreme cold. I still found it hard to wrap my mind around anything below minus 20 deg. C, but what happened next even I could identify with.

Ever seen a bunch of drug addicts go through withdrawal? It's not a pretty sight. I'd been rationing myself all week. I didn't have much tobacco left when I arrived in Porcupine, but since then I'd shared it all away. Now I was down to my last roller. One person was already into the tea bags and another was reduced to recycling butt ends. I have many vices, but only two practicing ones, eating and smoking. The former was no problem, the latter had me climbing the walls. One insensitive soul only added insult to injury by firing off statistics on life expectancy, brain damage and the passive smoke argument, but when he cast aspersions on our reduced libido and sperm count he came within a hair's breadth of being lynched.

By midnight it was all over. The blizzard had run its course and the following morning the Rangers left. I stayed on in the cabin, but by the fourth day 1 was heading out down Porcupine Bay en route to the Island of Ponds.

There is a saying on the Labrador coast that Black Tickle manufactures storms for export to the mainland, and my arrival there coincided with a major dig out. Black Tickle is an off-shore community of three hundred people located on the south west corner of the Island of Ponds. There's not a single twig or bush to be found anywhere, nothing, to soak up the 90 mile/hr winds that battered the settlement and as I walked down to the harbour its full force was plainly evident.

Mountainous snow drifts stuck to anything above ground level and filled in the rest. For the children it was a great excuse to toboggan, while for the adults it was a natural 'Make Work Project' of mega proportions. The first two houses I came to were buried up to their roof tops and, had I not seen puffs of snow coming out of an eight foot deep hole from another, I would have been none the wiser. Electricity and telephone lines were now at chest height and as I was soon to find out, had been used as life lines of evacuation during the blizzard "You couldn't see your hand in front of your face, Boy. The only way you could get around was by touch."

Stories came thick and fast. Black Tickle's power failed the first night and as two thirds of the houses have oil-fired central heating, by the second night mass evacuations were the order of the day. Whole families, dogs and cats included, crawled along from one power line to another searching out neighbours with wood-fired stoves. One house took in a dozen people, another with only three rooms took in over twenty, but not all families without power wanted to leave. Some just roughed it out with extra layers of clothing and candles. One enterprising family hooked up a bicycle to generate power and yet another, stubborn to the end, chopped up furniture to keep the stove going.

This blizzard wasn't even the first that year. In fact, I was told they were a regular part of life. The first question that came to mind was, why? Why do people live here?

For us mere mortals the term 'basic survival' has been dispatched to the history books, but here on the island they've breathed life back into the saying. For instance, what kind of person would put up with having to travel four miles for water and thirty miles for wood in the dead of winter? Let alone live through intermittent power failures, frozen pipes and a primitive sewage system that sometimes left you emptying buckets of waste on harbour ice.

In St. John's I heard the first stories of Black Tickle. "They're all Newfies who went there to fish in the summer and missed the last boat home in fall". On the surface you would think they were all crazy. Outside their modern airstrip, there is no other all-year round mode of transportation onto the mainland. During the summer months boats can be used and in winter ski-doos can cross the frozen waters of Porcupine Bay. But during the dangerous months in spring and fall when the ice is unsafe, they might as well be in Timbuktu.

To find the answer I had to look back to the '60's and Joey Smallwood's resettlement program. In those days places like Mary's Harbour, Port Hope Simpson, Charlottetown and Cartwright were just blimps on the map. The Labrador coast was still full of small communities, some hidden away in coves, some at the end of remote points of land and some, like Black Tickle, stuck to bare rock like limpets. Then came resettlement and overnight the inhabitants shut up shop and migrated to the mainland. Many over the years have returned. Some families use their old homes as summer cottages and move lock stock and barrel to be close to their fishing grounds and yet other buildings have turned into ghostly museums. Black Tickle was also given the option of resettlement. The younger generation voted to leave, but in those days major decisions were made by elders and the family heads of the Dyson and Keefes voted to stay, so they stayed.

By the end of the day the old Health Clinic had been converted into my home. The oil tank was topped up, electricity connected and apart from having to get my drinking water from a bucket and use the portable 'honey pot' for a toilet, I had all the amenities of home. Soon my rooms had turned into the local drop-in centre. A meal appeared, soft drinks and cookies. The night stretched into a revolving door of food and bodies, then somewhere along the line I let my guard down, relaxed into their hospitality, and uttered the dreaded four letter word 'FISH'.

"Fish, what bloody fish?" I'd opened a can of worms now there was nothing for it but listen and hope that they would remember my guest status.

"I didn't catch one cod this year", he put up a finger to emphasize the point. "not one. When I was a kid, I could catch ten times that off the wharf before breakfast. Two years ago you could walk across this harbour without wetting your feet. The harbour was chocka block full of fishing boats. You can ask anyone; Black Tickle was the place to be then, but I doubt if we will see one boat next year."

As one man waned another took up the story.

"Imagine you were choking on a fish bone, You knew it, but you couldn't get the words out. That's how I feel. Nobody listens to the patients. We've been analyzed to death, boy. Social workers, that's the only growth industry in these parts."

I didn't need a Ph.D in anthropology to understand what made them tick. Why they came and why they stayed. Sandwiched between the Atlantic and an endless coastal wilderness, their very existence and character had been molded by forces outside their command and now it sounded as if the government had got into the act too.

"Why do you think there's no fish?" I tried to get the topic back on track, away from politics and back to fish.

"Everything has its season." If I'd heard that phrase once I'd heard it a dozen times. "You just can't harvest year round. Fish needs time to breed."

A fish moratorium was in the air and its black cloud had followed me through every community. I never once heard sun-spot activities, ozone levels or black holes blamed for the in-shore fisheries decline.

"Over-fishing."

To these people it was as easy as that. Draggers, over quota dumping but, most of all, a technology gone crazy and driven on by greed. Once thriving coastal communities are now on the brink of collapse and the saddest problem is there's a whole new generation growing up with only government make-work pro grams to look forward to. The terms UI, STAMPS, WELFARE andMAKE-WORK PROGRAMS are part of everyday vocabulary. Kids are being born into a system of hand-outs and it's molding a character that will do without more before settling for less and that is downright criminal.

The night tailed off into one of those subjects you had to drop before it drowned you. I'd tried my best to deflect this question of fisheries before, but you can't hide from it for long when it dominates nearly every serious conversation on the coast. Even my visitors caught the mood and before midnight I was on my own again.

I'm the kind of fellow who can switch on and off my alcohol addiction as easy as a light switch. I've never suffered the shakes of withdrawal, seen pink elephants in my dreams or done mantras to a six pack. You need a clear head when travelling through a new experience and alcohol and concentration don't mix. Having said that there are always exceptions. Full moons are a good excuse, Jupiter in Saturn isn't bad either and Friday the 13ths are worth drinking to. Weddings have to be celebrated, funerals drowned and today being March 11th, my birthday, couldn't pass without some kind of substance abuse.

I stayed in Black Tickle for six days. I wanted to spend my 43rd birthday there. In the last twelve years I had spent eight of them on the road. This time I wanted to be around familiar faces for once, to close the door on travel, get drunk and let tomorrow take care of itself.

The big day was passing like a long pause. I was waiting for a ski-doo from Cartwright. Why, you may ask? Because Black Tickle is dry. Well, that's not totally true. You can always visit Hudson's Take-Out'and for the minimum service charge of fries and gravy buy one beer. A burger and fries allows you two and if you order from their a-la-carte menu the bar is yours. It all adds up to an expensive drunk that only your visiting politician or hydro worker can afford and is certainly not within the reach of your average penny pincher like myself. That left me with a big problem. Having made up my mind to get drunk, then found the door closed, Bernie was a frustrated little boy. I needed either a stroke of luck or divine intervention. I'd already pushed my luck to the limit, so I had to rely on the latter and divine intervention in Black Tickle had only one name: 'Hudson'.

You want to find the name George Hudson in the annals of Who's Who. Here on the coast the Hudsons and families like theirs are the real power brokers and rulers of Labrador, not the Queen of England, nor the Canadian Parliament nor the Premier in St. John's. On the island the Hudsons ran everything. They ran the fish plant, the hotel, the restaurant, the store and even a small private airline. It seemed that every time money changed hands it passed into their tills. And as most transactions were made via government cheques in their store, it meant they had the bank franchise as well. A formidable family to say the least, but I've always believed in going straight to the top and now I was hoping against hope that they'd heard of me.

"I'm the walking man."

"Who?" I'd played my trump card first, but his question cancelled me out. "You know, the guy who's walking up the coastline of Labrador."

Suddenly his eyes stood to attention. "Oh yeh, you're the one on television."

I was in. Seats were pulled out, and a Pepsi called for. My feet were firmly under the table. The order of beer was relayed by phone to Cartwright. A question in the right ear, a little back scratching and string pulling. It's as easy as that on the coast.

At 5:00pm I was still waiting. I'd heard down the grapevine that my beers had arrived from Cartwright, now I was worried my birthday was being celebrated elsewhere without me. It was now 7:00pm. The Sacred Heart teachers had cooked up a feast and we were half way through when my beers turned up. I had the first opened and emptied before its messenger had time to dust off his boots. That sealed the night. Bernie was a happy boy. By the second I had a slight crush on a teacher and by the third I was ready to enlarge it. The food was great, the conversation funny and at least one friendship was cemented. That night the beers cushioned my sleep and the following morning saw me up bright and early and ready to walk off its effects.

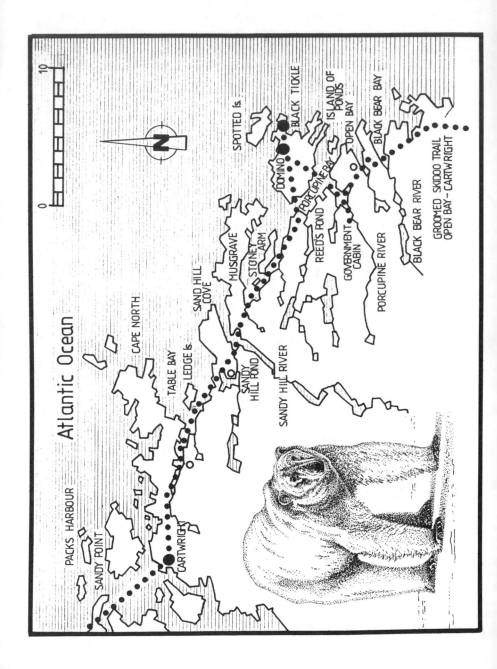

Chapter 9
Uproot and Transplant

MILES OF UNPROTECTED SHORELINE, wind-hardened surfaces and sea ice all add up to speedy travel. After seven restful days in Black Tickle I had itchy feet. Cartwright beckoned, but there was one problem - the weather.

A satellite dish in Labrador can be both a luxury and a hindrance. Media Literacy may be a second language in North American high schools, but here on the coast it is still in its infancy. Last night I had switched to the weather channel, only to be barraged with a screen full of computer readouts, predicted weather patterns and colour codes, which to the average Joe like myself meant nothing. I didn't know the jargon and to comprehend it fully needed either a doctorate in climatology or a pocket calculator. Outside the night was crisp and clear, while on the screen it showed a low pressure rapidly moving north from Texas on a collision course with an arctic front from northern Quebec. A speeded up computer version of these cloud formations moved across the screen at satellite distances, blotting out first the Central United States before invading Canada's East Coast and striking the arctic high near Halifax. It then deflected east, before swirling round the coastline of Labrador. I didn't like what I saw. But not being able fully to understand the information only added to my worries. Then, just as weather forecast was beginning to sink in, the picture changed and suddenly Australia popped up onto the screen.

I started the day off like an express train and now it was ending like a limp squib. For most of the day I set my own course. Black Tickle to the mainland was done in double quick time, Narrow Island came and went before noon and I had no problem picking my way across the frozen shallow waters of Stoney Arm. It was when I turned inland towards Sandy Hill that the weather caught me.

All day the temperature had climbed. 7:00am minus 15 deg.C, 9:00am minus 10deg.C, 11:00am ZERO deg.C. It rose in leaps and bounds and when the clouds closed in I braced myself for the inevitable. Rain, buckets full of it. It started as snow flurries, turned into raindrops and then sheeted down. The snow soaked up the rain like a sponge, but rocks exposed to the wind chill soon glazed. One pond swam with water and another, frozen with fresh ice, had me slip-sliding across it. By late afternoon the temperature had gone down with the sun and rain-drops now stuck to my clothing like armour plating. Underfoot the wind-hardened snow made walking easy, but my sled, more influenced by wind than any direction I could offer, had a mind of its own.

I was less than two miles away from Sandy Hill Government Cabin when I called it a day. The rain had turned to a fine mist. I was wet, cold and deject-ed, and more than anything I craved a fire.

Paper or birch bark, that was the question. At one time I would have used nothing but paper to light a fire, but then I had never before lit one in freezing rain. Birch bark has one important property that paper hasn't; it burns even when wet. It's no differ-ent than lighting an oil wick, it feeds off its own juices and once started there's no stopping it. The bark isn't difficult to harvest and peels off in the same way a snake exchanges old skin for new. It didn't take me long to find a tree, strip off some coils and ignite them. Soon they were spitting out small blobs of flame. Next came the twigs, great knotted piles of them. Flames went from red to amber to deep blue. Twigs yielded to branches, to dry logs and soon yel-low sparkles eddied skywards. I had just started to hang my wet socks and liners on twigs when the fire collapsed. Its base melted, then the rain returned.

Some days it doesn't pay to get out of bed and today was one of those days. My tent was a sheet of ice, socks froze as they fell and boot liners fused together. I was now reduced to my third-string mitts and my gortex wind proofers needed a good beating before any sense of flexibility returned. That was the good news, the bad news was that my tent poles were cemented together. I couldn't heat them, because their threaded cord would have melted. Instead, I had to painstakingly pick out the frost and by the time I broke camp the morning was half over.

Today was a ditto of yesterday. Mist, rain and a dull ache at the back of my head that told me it wasn't going to get any better. Scenery was now a poor second to human contact, but people were never around when I most needed them. The days were getting longer, the sun higher, but I would gladly have traded this dull March day for a clear, frigid one in February. To cut a long story short I was feeling sorry for myself, and when the fog rolled in down Table Bay I called it quits.

The shoreline was a mixture of staggered pressure ridges and smooth drifts. The fog cut down my options, but I could have tried harder. It was impossible to judge exactly where the bay ice finished and the shoreline started. Common sense told me to get out of this no-mans land, at the very least attach my camp to some tree up the bank, but no, I was too tired. I pitched my tent between drifts, cooked with my stove and was in dreamland before dark.

WANG, VUM, VUM, VUM, VUM.....

I was out of bed and into my trousers in seconds.

WANG, VUM, VUM, VUM, VUM.....

My flashlight caught it. A straight black line draining snow. The tide had dropped, buckled the ice, and cracked it like glass. I had guessed at the right side of the line, but only just. I spent the next ten minutes satisfying myself that I was safe then spent the rest of the night dreaming of earthquakes.

I woke to clear skies. The air was crisp and brittle. The two days of rain had packed the snow and an early morning frost had hardened its crust. The trees looked a little greener, the snow a little whiter and my steps had purpose and bounce. The groomer had just passed. Holes were filled in, drifts levelled and the surface packed and smoothed.

Table Bay tapered into a series of long narrow inlets and, combined with the oval ponds crossed later, joined the whole morning like a string of sausages. At the end of these frozen bodies of water the trail stepped up, funnelled between two hills, then opened to a spectacular view of the coast. Below, I could clearly make out the mouth of Sandwich Bay, its islands and, beyond, the open sea. Due north, a flat coastline gave way to a huge tidal wave of rock. It was my first view of the Mealey Mountains. They were awesome.

Before Mary's Harbour I had planned to branch off from Cartwright down Sandwich Bay to the settlement of Paradise River, follow the Eagle River into the foothills, cross the Mealey Mountains, hook up with the Kenemich River and follow it down to Lake Melville. Until today the idea of climbing over the mountains was just an idea, now it was definitely on hold. Just the thought made my stomach swim. But the more I stared at the huge barrier of white crests the more its germ took hold. I know my limits, but I also knew that with a little more planning and experience the trek over the mountains was there for the taking.What an adventure. Man against the elements, no ski-doos, no human contact. I knew right then I wouldn't turn my back on Labrador without giving it a try, but that's another story.

From here it was all downhill. Cartwright was just around the corner. I could almost touch it. My mouth was starting to saliva from the thought of home cooked bread and I could almost smell the perfume of fresh clean sheets. I was in a rush. I didn't see the warning signs. The man made snow bank, the

parked school bus. I hadn't looked both ways since
Toronto. I was lucky, damn lucky. I slipped on the
snow bank, fell onto my sled and tobogganed straight
in front of an oncoming car. One silent motor vehicle
and dozens of noisy ski-doos, that's progress for you.

Cartwright's distinction of being the only coastal
community owning a snow plough and year round
road didn't end there. It wasn't its size, although its
population of 600 plus put it second only to Nain as
the coasts most populous settlement. It wasn't its
services, either, even though it was home to a who's
who of government facilities including a R.C.M.P.
Detachment, Fish and Wild Life offices, Volunteer
Coast Guards, a Nursing Station, the second largest
High School on the coast, newest Hotel, largest
Airport and a Deep Water Harbour second to none.
Impressive as these statistics sound it was its pot-
pourri of resettled families that stood out the most.

If you believe what you read in the newspapers,
Toronto and Vancouver have cornered the market on
multiculturalism. Islam, Sikh turbans and Somalia
refugees are a fact of life these days. It's easy to over
look the fact that you don't have to come from another country, be black, disabled or homosexual to have
a social problem. Imposed resettlement caused all the
above in Cartwright, and in the process stretched its
facilities to the breaking point and pushed Labrador's
brotherly love to the limit. Before resettlement in the
'60's Cartwright was mostly home to the Birds,
Martins and Pardys. That was before the Williams
family was uprooted from North River, Winters from
Muddy Bay, Browns from Separation Point, Meshers
from Paradise River, Lethbridges and Learnings from
Eagle River, Reeves from Hare Harbour, Elsons from
Spotted Island, Dysons and Webbers from Batteau
and Holwells from Porcupine Bay. It all added up to
a strange mixture, the type romantic fiction novels
leave off at the beginning which is always the end of
fictional adventures.

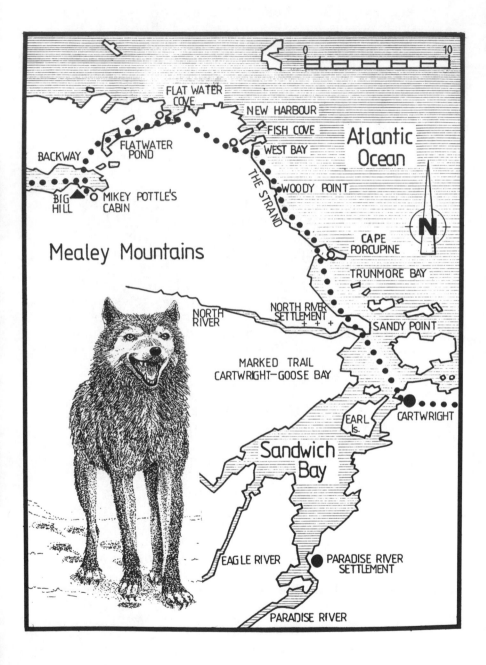

Chapter 10
Back Way's Unique Character

HOW PLEASANT IT WOULD BE TO LET THE sun get up without me. When it was minus 28 deg. C. I wasn't in a rush, but once the sun rose it warmed me up quickly. It turned out to be a beautiful morning. Crystal clear, with that long transparency that gives you telescopic vision. In the distance the horizon shimmered. The whole bay danced and glittered and by late morning the only relief my eyes got was the dark green wooded shoreline ahead. I had left Cartwright at 6:30am to cross the eight miles of Sandwich Bay to North River and didn't stop until I reached the river's settlement of summer cottages three hours later. I couldn't ask for a better start. I rested, had a brew-up, snapped on my snow shoes then broke trail over the short Sandy Point to Trunmore Bay.

From here the trail cut a path through an amazing landscape of sea ice. Pressure ridges rose and fell and their sharp edges caught the sun's rays like a thousand panes of broken glass. Ice pressed in and up around submerged rocks and took on the form of mini-volcanos. Rusty coloured sea slob stained nearly every point of shoreline. The further I wandered out into the bay the smoother the surface and soon my only companions were the groans of ice as different levels rubbed up against the tide.

I was now travelling on an exposed shoreline, which on ski-doo is no problem but by foot can play havoc on the nerves. On one hand there was the open sea and on the other a low level shoreline, shaved by an easterly wind that hid its outline under a continuous snow drift. If a storm came now-and I'd learned not to trust the weather -there was no escape. I could only go forward to Cape Porcupine or back to Sandy

Point. True, I had a compass, but the ice corridor of bay ice didn't leave much room for error. I didn't like the idea of walking on water or sinking into sea slob. So, not for the first time, I put haste above sight seeing and anchored my eyes on Cape Porcupine and started the long pull in.

When exhaustion comes, it comes quickly. I just made land when my legs gave out. Left alone all day, my mind had jumped onto a different plane. I thought of nothing else but crossing the bay. I had been in perpetual motion for three hours. Now the spell was broken. Heat turned to cold, dull aches to biting pain and fatigue to breakdown. One moment the sky was clear, the next jet black. I passed out. My head burned and I had a lump on it the size of a prune, but thankfully no blood. I had dipped below my reserves. I was a wreck, but two chocolate bars later my senses returned.

Strange things happen at night when your guard is down and that's why I kept a fire going as long as possible. During the day I could push thoughts of accidents and polar bears to the back of my mind, but at night they came out with a vengeance. To cover myself against accidents I carried a survival kit the envy of any doctor and for protection against polar bears I slept with a shot gun like a security blanket. Still, having and using are two different worlds, and a false sense of security is sometimes worse than the threat itself.

That night I didn't sleep well. I knew something was out there, but while the embers crackled I feared nothing. Twice I got up, twice I shone the flashlight around. Nothing, and by the third time it was close to dawn. This time it was for definite. I could hear an animal breathing, then scratching noises. SHIT..........

Two white pools of light shone back at my flashlight. CLICK! Nothing, no sound, no kick, no slug. Not even a silent prayer. A gun is a great equalizer when loaded, but as useless as a piece of tin when not. There wasn't much else left for me to do except swear. Needless to say, I'm still alive. Whatever it was, it wasn't a polar bear, but I didn't take any chances. There was no way I was going back inside the tent before a fire was lit and when I woke it was still smoldering.

My nose is my most reliable barometer, but this morning it was my head. The prune had shrunk to a grape, but my hangover told a different story. It was frigid. A stiff breeze blew in from the sea and the horizon was a foaming crest of clouds.

I was now travelling on a coastal corridor known locally as the Strand. Local knowledge was full of short cuts, but the track of sea ice from Cape Porcupine to West Bay looked dangerous and, coupled with the threat of a storm, made me hug the shore. I was now trusting less what people said and more my own judgement. Only in the depths of winter, I had been told, were conditions stable A safe spot today may be sure death tomorrow. Recent weather had been freakish. Swings from minus 28 deg.C to plus 6 deg.C and rain to snow on alternate days did nothing for my confidence. Brooks opened and closed overnight and their layers of decker ice were becoming a continual problem.

There are many reasons for decker ice. Overhangs may collapse under the weight of snow and then refreeze at different levels. Same with ice jams, and rain is a law unto itself. The reasons are numerous and the only safe way to cross a brook is to look and listen and if you are still unsure, check with an axe. Finally I had bought one and as the Strand empties numerous brooks, it soon paid for itself.

I found no rhythm to the day. Brook slob froze on contact and I had a fulltime job chipping the ice of my sled runners. More than once I got my feet wet and in the end I wrapped both in cooking foil. By late afternoon the wind changed to a south westerly. Temperatures soared and the snow stuck like cobwebs to my leggings. Two miles before West Bay the ski-doo trail lipped over the shoreline, climbed up its banks and levelled out onto a frozen marsh. The sky had emptied and the air was motionless. A gully split the trail ahead like a defense ditch.

The sun was setting quickly and there was an urgency to my steps. To the east, woods tapered off into a group of low hills and to the west, shelter was barricaded behind a thick thatch of willows. I wasted too much time and energy looking for a suitable camp site, then a shallow gully breached the problem and I found my spot. The sun had already dropped below the tree line. Colour was fading fast. I erected the tent in double quick time, then watched the moon rise. A blue moon. Maybe it was my imagination. The moon looked like a huge circular mirror, and as it rose the shadows swung round to greet it. I could now turn my attention to a fire. The moon's light turned the countryside into a lunar landscape of pale white and I had no trouble collecting firewood.

Now that I had an axe I could build a proper fire. Meltdown had always been a problem, but now I could prevent it with a raft of green logs. I loved everything about fires, the wood collection, the lighting, its smell, look and especially toasting my buns after a long day. If it wasn't for the uniforms and discipline I would have signed up as a fire fighter straight from school. I was one of those borderline pyromaniacs who could never put a match box down until it was empty. I looked forward to these periods of fire building, especially my first hot mug of tea.

As I've Mentioned, tea is something akin to a religion in these parts and the partaking of is nothing less than a religious experience. Just consider a piping hot stove, the humid hiss of boiling water and the chatter of friendly voices. Coming from England, I've always been an addict, but tea stewed in a smoke-stained pot balanced on a twig over an open fire in snow, sugar by the spoons full and drunk while sitting on a carpet of sweet smelling balsam boughs is the best tea of all. There are not many advantages to being single, but this experience was one of them.

I'd learned my camping and fire technique by trial and error - to make a mat of boughs for insulation, to shovel snow against the side of the tent, to use green wood for a fire platform and, most importantly, to light fires before making and breaking camp.

It was hours after dark. Above, the northern lights were dancing and in the distance, I could hear the deep-throated muffled sounds of a ski-doo. For once, I slept half-in and half-out of the tent. The fire was dying. Flames extinguished and fell inwards with a soft cindery sound, and yellow sparks illuminated my tent. It was time to turn in. Somewhere along the line, the air turned sticky. C.B.C. shortwave crackled, wavered in and out, then skipped stations. A coastal weather forecast turned into African calypso music, to reggae, then to hockey results. Two incidents don't a storm make, but when I woke to a haloed sunrise, the writing was on the wall.

Today was to be a short one. My plan was to make Flat Water Cove and rest up in a know cabin. That was the plan, but it didn't work out that way.

I hadn't even broken camp when I experienced one of Labrador's notorious weather changes. In ten minutes a wind shift swung 180 degrees from southwest to northeast. Temperatures dropped and clouds darkened, but when a fine mist of snow descended and hill tops disappeared, I knew trouble was just around the corner. A lone wolf crossed my path and was soon lost to the woods, and within seconds so were its trees. At first the snow was damp, giant flakes, then came the wind and as the morning drew on the temperature dropped. By noon the snow had agreed with the wind and drifted in perfect sheets. The landscape was closing in fast and when the trail opened out into the cove everything washed together into a white blur.

The storm in the morning was a tea party compared to the one that greeted me now. The frost stung my breath, stabbed into my lungs and cut into my flesh. There was no facing it and periodically I had to walk backwards to give my face a rest. I'd set my compass for the cabins at the other side of the bay but I never found them. Instead, I ended up camping in the first cluster of trees I came across.

I woke to find my camp ankle deep in slob. The high tide had forced its way through the ice up the shallow bank and was now sponging its way through the snow. Had I not put down a carpet of boughs under my tent everything would have been soaked. I broke camp and immediately found another on higher ground, lit a fire and dried out.

It's at times like these that one takes stock of the situation and common sense prevails, but Bernie is made from a different mold. After eight weeks of breaking trail up the coast, I had this almost unshakable belief that nothing bad could happen to me, so going against all the signs telling me to stay, I broke camp only to be lost instantly to the storm.

For the next six hours I ploughed through powdered dust, sometimes walking backwards, sometimes crawling on all fours. I was travelling through a corridor of inches, up Flatwater Brook. Hood down, I could barely squint through its inch-wide slit. Snow cut like needles and the wind forced its grains down my neck. Since morning I had been semi-lost. The scattered ski-do track, nailed-up gas cans and compass kept my spirits up, but only just. I was on a razor edge and any moment fear could get the upper hand. In a storm you feel very much alone. It's like swimming underwater. A sudden drop in wind and you surface, get your bearings, take a breath, then the curtain of storm drops and you're underwater again. Twice I almost lost it. Once was when I read my map wrong and ended up waist deep in a birds' nest of woven branches, but by far the worst took me to the bottom of a cone-shaped snowdrift. . Suddenly the surface gave way. My left leg buckled, passed my shoulder on the way down and came to rest above my head. At first I thought it was broken, but then a jerk of life, a smack of pain and it damn near broke my nose.

I was now quite high. Flatwater Pond was behind me and it was still snowing, but when the wind dropped, colour and calm returned. The world fell into place, landmarks lit up like beacons, but no sooner had I checked my bearings than the wind blew away the picture and the struggle returned. I continued at a snail's pace up to a point where the winds flattened me. I was on the crest of a hill. Here I assumed correctly that I must be overlooking Back Way and a drop in wind made it reality.

There is an old saying, 'God looks after His chosen people', or as my mother put it, 'His chosen fools'. Big Hill, that large pyramid of rock and trees that for generations of travellers has acted as a beacon of portage across Back Way, was in plain view and as the wind dropped further the lazy curve that outlined Deep Cove's throat underlined my position.

So close yet so far away. I was exhausted. My feet were like jelly and the wind so noisy I couldn't hear myself think. It just wouldn't let up and the further I dropped into the cove the slipperier the surface became. The last view I remember was from my bum. The sled tipped, caught the wind, clipped my ankles and then dragged me along like a water skier. 100ft-50ft- 20ft-10ft-OUCH!

If only I could have seen where I was going I would have enjoyed it. Half way down I entered the twighlight zone of snow dust and when I hit bottom I couldn't see my hand in front of my face. It was like being caught in a wind tunnel. Snow or sand, you couldn't tell. Instant blindness. Eyes watered, froze and watered again. Wind blasts struck and downed me as surely as leg trips. Hidden snow drifts left me spread-eagled and polished ice, on all fours. I was black and blue from knee to elbow before I'd got halfway. It's a good thing I was 100% certain that

shelter lay just across the cove. I'd burned my
bridges. Life signs were fading. I seemed to have
developed an in-built immune system against total
collapse. I was soaked but didn't feel wet and one
side of my face had turned to putty, a sure sign of
frost bite. Defeat, as my dad use to say, is never ter-
minal unless you give up, and no one could call me a
quitter. Forty five minutes later I was staring down a
C.B. antenna.

"So you're the walking man! My name's Mikey
Pottle. Come in and warm up, me boy."

There are certain people who, either through their
unique character, or chance meeting, stand out from
the rest and Mikey Pottle is one of them. A castback
to the old traditional days when working men wore
white canvas dickies, sealskin mukluks and snow-
shoed everywhere, he's a short wiry man whose fea-
tures have been toned and hardened through years of
exposure to the outdoor life. Now in the autumn of
his years, his life has taken a direction that rubs
against the tide of RRSP's, plastic surgery and sun
worship; he has chosen to return to his birthplace at
the bottom of Back Way, rather than going to Florida
to spend the winter months. Due to his cabin's location just off the coastal ski-doo trail, it had become,
over the years, quite literally the drop-in centre for
both tired weary travellers and for those lost souls
who, like myself, occasionally get trapped out in
storms.

I first heard the name Mikey Pottle in Port Hope
Simpson, again in Black Tickle and by the time I
reached Cartwright Mikey Pottle had grown into a
living legend, if not the holder of every kind of gossip
and dark secret on the coast. So you can imagine my
excitement in wanting to meet the guy.

You would never see Mikey's home televised in
The Rich and Famous or read about it in the pages of
Home Improvement. It was a bare skeleton compared
to the norm but like its owner it carried no surface fat.
I found in Mikey and his live-in girlfriend Rachel

Palisser two people who, like myself, delighted in the fundamental hardships of nature. They preferred hard beds to soft ones, the extremes of climate to those governed by technology and a lifestyle bound to the rise and fall of the seasons.

For the longest time I said nothing. Exhaustion and excitement stuck the words in my throat. I couldn't even straighten my back, and chose a corner of the floor next to the stove in lieu of a chair. Life returned slowly. I'd get a sudden surge of energy, peel off a layer of clothes then collapse back into my corner. This yo-yo recovery took over an hour, and by supper I had covered every nail, hook and twine with damp clothes and as the evening meal disappeared Mikey's one-room cabin filled with the musky smell of Bernie's steamy sweat.

No sooner had my body normalized than my face erupted. A tell-tale itch, then a burning sensation and before retiring my head had caught fire. Frostbite is a common as sunburn, but that was of little comfort. I woke to find my cheeks red and raw, my nose scabbed and my right eye stuck shut with pus. An ignominious start to the day. My heart wasn't in travel. I left just after sunrise but was back at Mikey's before nightfall. I made it only as far as Main Brook, gave in to a cup of tea, joined a group ice fishing and then returned with my tail between my legs. If I was disappointed at my lack of mileage I shouldn't have been. Had I not returned I would have missed out on one of Labrador's oldest lifestyles: trapping. There was a dead martin hung up behind the door, its neck broken. Next to it was a freshly snared rabbit. I'd seen and tasted both before, but its life and death cycle had never been so close to home. The dead martin was the same one I had seen playing at breakfast from the kitchen table and the rabbit we were to eat for supper was still warm. Mikey trapped and killed animals like a farmer raises and butchers his livestock. It's what put a roof over his head and food on the table. We'd call it a job, he'd call it a way of life.

I woke to a polished bronze sunrise. Back Way was still under shadow, but its corridor of hills was a blaze of orange, yellow and gold. I should have left on an upbeat note, but I didn't. Mikey had been glad of an audience and I made a good listener. Friendship, openness and good humor had become part and parcel of these meetings, but that was the problem, I had to let go. I was becoming a nomad, an outsider looking in. I had slipped to the fringes of life, and for the first time I was getting weary. I said my goodbyes to Mikey and Rachel, braved out a smile then filed my feelings away until another day.

'SNOW FLURRIES.' I hate it when the weather forecaster uses this term. For your average North American it conjures up pictures of flakes falling as if on a Bing Crosby Christmas set. It's just a romantic fairy tale put out by Walt Disney. In Labrador a snow flurry may only last sixty minutes, but its effect may last for days. That six lane highway of hard packed snow I'd been promised down Back Way was somewhere under two days of powdered snow. I'd not heard one ski-doo in three days and if the snow kept up I wouldn't see one for many more. I was now walking on the second most travelled route on the coast and there wasn't a clue, or hint of a track anywhere. By noon my progress had dropped to a snail's pace. The wind had died, but the flurries were still coming. Flakes as big as your finger tips floated down and piled up like an unstoppable white tide. My snow shoes were useless. I was plowing through calf deep in white powder and by early afternoon I'd given up, exhausted. I made only six miles.

It would have been the kiss of death to continue. I was damp. All morning my body heat had melted the snow flakes and my sweater soaked it up. Now, when the wind struck, the frost bit and my body rattled. I made camp in double quick time, lit a fire, stripped and exchanged damp clothes for dry. The snow was still falling long after dark. It slid off my tent like sand

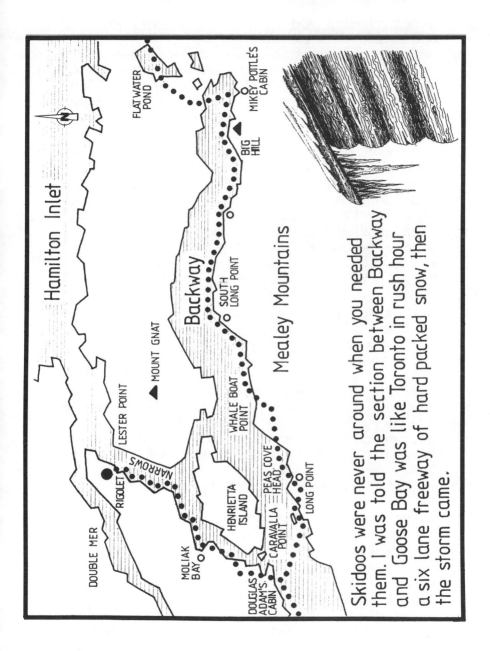

Skidoos were never around when you needed them. I was told the section between Backway and Goose Bay was like Toronto in rush hour a six lane freeway of hard packed snow, then the storm came.

paper, collected in deep drifts, pushed in the sides and cocooned me for the night.

Morning brought with it not only a major dig-out but a big headache. I'd lost count of the points of land I'd passed since Mikey's place. Shallow bays all look the same and their arteries of rivers and brooks were too deeply buried to spot. I was worried about the bad ice ahead and the two portages I had to take. It was a lousy morning. The sun was nonexistent and the only thing in my favor was that the temperature had plummeted, always a good sign that the snow would hold off. It did, but as so often happens after a big snowfall, there was now a wind storm. Unlike their big brother the blizzard, windstorms don't carry fresh snow, but recycle the old. All morning the snow billowed, bust and shot past like rockets. I was being worn down like soap stone. My face, blistered from the blizzard, started to peel and my nose was already on its second layer of skin.

I was trying my best to keep a straight course, but was wary of straying too far from shore. I was still trying to match contour lines with my map and clearings with known cabins. Each point of land had to be portaged, each clearing looked into. The corridor of hills all looked same and my compass reading could have put me in more than one location. I wasn't overly worried. I had plenty of fuel and food and if need be, I'd just camp and wait it out until a ski-doo passed. Then, just as the jigsaw puzzle in the form of Mount Gnat fell into place, the heavens flooded with noise.

WAP...WAP...WAP...WAP...WAP...WAP...WAP...

It was the Air Sea Rescue. They caught me on a break. I was sitting down in an armchair of snow, coffee mug in one hand, cigarette in the other. The first thing that popped into my head was, 'Where am I?'

At $400.00 per hour the Air Sea Rescue have little time for polite conversation. They are taught to think on the run and act in a flash and no sooner had the helicopter landed when the R.C.M.P. jumped out.

"Have you seen two ski-doos?" If he hadn't looked so serious it would have been funny

"NO". Here I was on my own, semi-lost, and on foot. I doubt if I had covered eight miles since breakfast and they were asking me for help. I was tonguetied. My mind was still wrapped around the mechanical bird in the snow, let alone formulating those all-important questions that popped in and out of my head. It all happened too quickly and when the offer of a ride to Goose Bay needed an answer, it slipped by without sticking . The visit was over before it really started and I was left more alone than ever before.

The feeling didn't last long. Mount Gnat's landmark located Paradise Bay, then came a cabin, the woodcut and the portage I was looking for. The icing on the cake came only moments later. A black caterpillar came into view, twisted, turned, then broke into four ski-doos. I was home and dry.

People on the trail are scarce and precious, particularly in dirty weather and soon I was making camp in a disused log cabin near Whale Boat Point and surrounded by familiar faces from Cartwright. After the brief encounter with Air Sea Rescue, it was nice to meet a laid-back group of characters. Their gifts of banana cake, fresh bread and molasses tongued charm were welcome reminders of what life is all about on the coast and by the time they left some hours later, I was well tucked in for the night.

My friends were en route to Rigolet so I would only have to follow their trail today. Right? Wrong. It snowed during the night so I was back to square one. I was so sure of their trail, I had paid little attention to their route description. so now it was back to the drawing board, counting points, following contours and hoping my compass readings were better than yesterday's.

It was your typical schizophrenic March day. Snow, rain and hail with just the right mixture of warm sun and biting cold to make selecting clothes a nightmare.

While the sun was low it was cold but as it rose so did the temperature and by noon the snow had become wet and sticky. The snows crust held till 10:00 am, then melted rapidly and by 11:00am the fresh snow was balling between my boots and snow shoe webbing. I had to stop repeatedly and pick it out by hand. It was driving me crazy. It felt like walking on pebbles, but worse was to come. At noon, the snow turned to junk.

On a scale of one to ten. Two steps stuck like glue, three glided and five crashed through the snow's icy crust into a knee deep no-man's land of powder called 'junk' that even snow shoes couldn't hold up in. Progress was down to a crawl. The only thing in my favor was the window of light. I'd just passed what I had taken for a point of main land when a tell tale shadow illuminated yesterday's ski-doo track over Lake Melville. Everything now fell into place. The blur ahead turned into Long Point, the slab of rock on the opposite shore into Henrietta Island and the Narrows, the gap of no-man's land between. I had found the crossing to Rigolet

Damn the weather. I'd just crossed the point of no return when the clouds rolled back, the sun shut down and it started to snow. When the wind started to scream across lake ice, I knew it wasn't my day. Here I was tramping through huge wave-like snow drifts, their tops glazed and wind-hardened and their bases stained and sticky, filled with dangerous tidal slob. If that wasn't bad enough, my vision was shutting down. I was travelling up a corridor between two points of land. To the east, less than one mile away, was a tidal rip of open water called the Narrows, which, if I fell into it,would carry my body down to Rigolet faster than I could run. To the west was a ninety mile deep strip of ice called Lake Melville which, if I strayed into it ,could swallow me up for days. Not a pleasant thought.

I'm not a religious man. I don't pray, believe in an after life or reincarnation. I weigh up my chances and go for it. But when the snow stopped and I came face to face with a green band of open water, I knew somebody up there liked me. By mid afternoon I had completed the steep portage by ski-doo trail over to Caravalla Bay.

If I ever had doubts about my day's efforts or my decision to make a detour through Rigolet, the sight of open water put them to rest. The Narrows lived up to all the pre-trip hype and then some. After two months of frozen bondage, to be walking only feet away from fast moving tidal sea water was an amazing sensation. Even the cold could not lock away its smell, and the subtle green colour of the water was a sight for sore eyes. Its surface was dotted with brilliant white and blue ice pans, some as large as football pitches. The whole scene was enhanced by steep banks of healthy forest and the sound of ice grinding on ice in the fast flowing eddies sent shivers down my back. Lake Melville was emptying. The natural plug, called a falling tide, had been pulled and ice pans were being drawn through the Narrows like a magnet towards the ocean.

I was now travelling on a fifteen feet wide bellicater. Until today the word 'bellicater' had just been a dictionary term used for 'ice frozen to land.' Now I was experiencing it first hand. Some places were almost impossible to traverse and on more than one occasion my heart jumped into my mouth. Thirty degree slopes may be no problem for ski-doos, but to a babe of sub-arctic experience like myself they were nightmares. Footing wasn't the problem, I could always find some purchase in ice cracks or snow, but my sled had a mind of its own. It refused everything but the shortest rein, sliding round at right angles when the slope dropped away and sometimes, when caught by sharper angles, dangled dangerously close to the water.

It's not my habit to take stupid risks, but children

aren't the only ones who can laugh at danger. I could-
n't resist trying my luck on a small ice pan. It was like
jumping on a huge raft, with one vital difference as
became immediately evident.   You move when it
moves and halt when it halts. I'd not taken into consideration that my movements on it would set off a
chain reaction that would release my ice raft from its
neighbors.   At first I thought I was in control, but
when my ski pole snapped pushing off against another ice pan I knew I'd lost the battle and had it not
kissed another ice floe I could have reached Rigolet
before I planned. A quick hop, skip and jump and I
was ashore. It wasn't a moment too soon.   The ice
pan circled an eddy, caught the current, and was gone
within minutes.

The unseasonable heat brought with it another
problem: 'decker ice'. Small streams of thaw now
froze in the dull light. I couldn't make out good ice
from bad and on more than one occasion I put my
foot through a thin layer of ice only to see it disappear
through another layer before I could switch weight to
my other leg.

Spring was in the air. Snowbirds clustered around
borders of last year's wild corn, harvesting the grain
in orgies of eating and completely oblivious to my
progress only yards away.   I was on the crest of a
wave and could have made Rigolet by nightfall but
at Moliak Bay I was seduced by an open cabin and
decided to spend a quiet night watching ice pans
under moonlight.

Chapter 11
A Trilogy of Memories

S HE SMILED AT ME AND INSTANTLY I WAS happy. Two drops of homebrew and I was in a different world. The floor turned to jelly and the walls started to slide. Everything looked suspect. The old saying 'You cannot separate a man from his landscape' is correct as far as it goes, but when you're seven sheets to the wind - in unfamiliar territory with a pretty lady - landscape means dally all. I should have stopped right there, but after two glasses I had gained a taste for it. My arrival in Rigolet had coincided with the Levi Pottle Memorial dog race and I found myself celebrating with the winning team, or was it runners up? At one point during the night's festivities I found myself outside taking a leak only to return to the wrong house. No problem, duplicate parties were going on everywhere. No sooner had I crossed the threshold when space was made, a seat was pulled up and a mountain of food materialized in front of me. I had already eaten my fill earlier. In fact, I could barely lift his eyes to the offering, let alone eat it.

"No, I couldn't possibly, love."

If looks could kill. I had just committed a cardinal sin. My words fell through the void of silence like an insult. I had to back peddle big time

"Just kidding." 'No' is the wrong word for a guest in a Labrador kitchen when food is being offered, especially when it's being underlined with a drink. Somewhere I found space, then washed it down with a few beers. What happened next is just a blur. Somehow I made it back to the Pottle household, found the correct bedroom and managed to hit the mattress and not the floor when I fell.

Three events in Rigolet stand out in my memory: the monsoon rains,the darts league and the church auction. The first I'm sure was for my benefit to keep me there. Not since Burma had I experienced such a prolonged downpour. At its height it sounded like metal pellets striking the roof. The sky was almost black, but it was noon. It lasted for two days, pushed the snow banks down by two feet and revealed a winter of lost ski-doo parts, submerged cars and rows of fences. It also kept the dogs quiet, people indoors, and ignited family fights over the rights to the T.V. remote. During this period I divided my time evenly between the kitchen, television and bedroom and when the rain finally stopped the burst of activity that followed was all one-way to the community centre and the weekly darts league.

The game of darts is more than just a sport on the coast, it's a way of life.You don't need to take steroids, wear protective clothing or break into a sweat. You can outfit yourself for the price of $30.00. It's a level playing field that transcends age barriers and brings together both sexes without fear for the birth rate. Its deity is a circular black and gold checked board and its rewards are the numerous plaques and statuettes that adorn many a household cabinet. In Cartwright they boasted having the best team on the coast, yet at Charlottetown's winter games I witnesseda man from Pinsent's Arm winning everything in sight. In Black Tickle you couldn't escape their black and gold colours and here in Rigolet it was the highlight of the week.

I had no problem getting invited to the league night. Being born in England has a certain mystique attached to it. After all, didn't we invent the game? Maybe my friends in Rigolet thought I had some inborn gifts. Balance, a certain flick of the wrist or, like a pitcher in baseball, perhaps it was my follow-through. Had I been born in Hongkong, I would have been relegated to that of spectator status and, immediately following my first three darts, that was where I wish they'd put me.

I just wasn't prepared. I had expected a quiet game between friends; instead, I had entered something akin to the mass hysteria of a Latin American carnival. High fives were the order of the day. "ON FIRE", "WAY TO GO", "GOT AN EYE", "FISH".

People were being cheered and jeered and overlapping whoops of joy were echoing from all four corners. You would think I could hide behind the noise. Wrong. Every time Bernie got up the room fell silent. "QUARTER!" I couldn't believe my score. The sum total of my three darts was seven.

"QUARTER!" Apparently anyone scoring less than 11 in three darts had to pay twenty five cents. Things went from bad to worse. The next game, I got skunked (a term used for anyone not been able to start off with a double before the game finished). We were playing a game called 1001 and had I been left to score it all on my own, I would be in Rigolet to this day. The night wasn't a total loss. The excitement swept me up and as the smoke got thicker and the dart board more distant I managed to win one. Well, not a dart game. It was the raffle, and I won a dozen beers.

The final trilogy of memories played itself out some days later with the Anglican Church Auction. It was one of the major events of the year and everybody participated in one way or another. It was standing room only at the community centre. The raucous auction had little in common with its more genteel cousin, Sotheby's of London, but what it lacked in Renoirs and Ming Dynasty china it more than made up for in colour and variety.

The stage was full to overflowing. It had everything from teddy bears to flash lights, pocket knives to tea sets, but it was the hand made local handicrafts that most people came to bid on. There were two sets of seal skin gloves, one seal skin hat, seal skin mukluks, moose hide slippers, a canvas dickie, a pair of snow shoes, hook rugs, sweet grass mats and numerous knitted garments. The pride of place on the stage went to a full-sized wooden komatik. However the most often visited place was the complimentary tea and coffee table on the floor.

Bidding was fast and furious.Cheers and applause followed every sale and the game was more in the chase than the actual prize. The school teachers cornered the market on the handicrafts and the locals the rest. I was after a pair of sealskin gloves. I could have waited till Goose Bay to buy a pair, but I'd set my heart on entering the bidding game and no matter what the price I wanted to leave some money behind in Rigolet for all the good times it gave me. At last the gloves were paraded round the room. The bidding started at thirty dollars and quickly went to eighty dollars. By now there were only three of us left; myself, a teacher and someone from the stage who I couldn't quite make out.

"Eighty Dollars."

"Eighty one dollars."

"Eighty five dollars."

"Eighty six dollars."

"Ninety dollars."

"Ninety one dollars." My opponents were going up in ones and fives and just as the auctioneer got to 'going twice', I'd round the figure off with a zero. At one hundred and twenty dollars, there were two of us left. The teacher had dropped out. "One hundred and thirty dollars."

"One hundred and thirty one dollars."

"One hundred and forty dollars."

"One hundred and forty one dollars."

"One hundred and fifty dollars."

"One hundred and fifty one dollars." Each bid was counter bid, but as the price climbed, my opponent wavered. I was in hook, line and sinker. I had two hundred and fifty dollars on me. The gloves were only worth eighty dollars tops, but who cares when you're having fun?

"One hundred and eighty dollars." I turned the screws and pushed the price up by twenty nine dollars. There was a long pause. All eyes turned to the stage. The vicar looked like a battered prize fighter, hanging on more out of pride then hope.

Good god, the vicar! Until that moment, I hadn't been able to put a name to the face on the stage. I had been bidding all this time, pushing up the price, knowing I could and would go up to two hundred and fifty dollars and all the time dragging the vicar behind me. How could he refuse? This was his flock, his wife had bid and bought him a sealskin hat. Now it was his turn. He had set out to bid on the same pair of women's sealskin gloves as I had. For ten minutes, I though I'd been a hero, now I felt like a villain. The crowd was willing him on, and secretly, so was I.

"One hundred and eighty one dollars.

The vicar chocked out the bid, the crowd erupted, and I let out a sigh of relief. The onlookers didn't know, but I did. It was over and when I started to clap my hands, everyone joined in. The vicar got his women and she got her gloves.

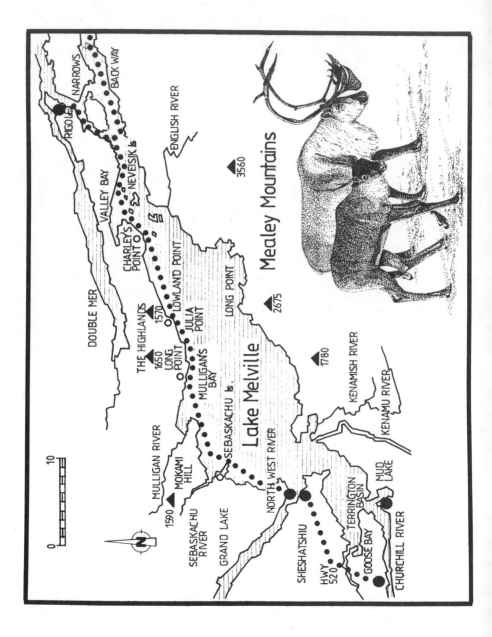

Chapter 12
An Endless Expanse of Ice

I COULD HAVE STAYED IN BED, BUT THAT damn ego of mine was chasing another story. Outside, winter was having its final fling. Snow was blowing horizontally and Rigolet was up to its armpits. I was now entering my final chapter. I didn't want to hang about thinking of Goose Bay, or where I could stay. I had another 90 miles to cover. The more I thought of Lake Melville's endless expanse of ice, the more daunting the mileage became.

It took me eight hours to cover what less than a week ago took me two. The Bellicater down the Narrows was knee deep in snow. My sled, so smooth to pull on the wind hardened coastal surfaces, now sunk as if in a bog. I was reduced to relaying, first breaking a trail with my snow shoes, then returning to pull the sled over its footprints. It was slow work, but infinitely better than a back-breaking plow through virgin snow.

Doug Saunder's cabin in Caravalla Cove couldn't come soon enough and when I woke the next morning to find it still snowing, it took a monumental battle of wills to prize myself loose from its one-room coziness.

By 8:00 a.m. I had dropped on to Lake Melville. After the weeks of uneven marshes, barrens, woodcuts and steep banks, I could now appreciate a level pulling surface. The wind had corrugated the fresh snow into tiny drifts and the single-digit temperatures were helping to settle it. The sled now moved smoothly behind, and even with snow shoes, I soon found a rhythm. I was on automatic pilot. My eyes were focused on Shag Island and my mind released to wander. Then suddenly out of the gloom came a dark object. At first I thought it was a broken-down ski-doo. It was jet-black, half a mile ahead and just off the heading I was travelling on. Then it moved, stopped, and moved again. It wasn't a wolf and it was too thickset to be a caribou. The closer it got, the more it looked like a bear. It had that rippling roly-poly movement that discounted every other scenario I could think of.   Could the mild weather have spoiled its alarm clock? I know bears don't completely hibernate, but why was it on the ice? I stopped and waited to see which way it would go. Five minutes passed, it was getting closer and still coming in my direction. I was starting to feel the first twinges of alarm. I set about looking for my binoculars, but came up with my gun. I loaded , aimed skyward and fired. Nothing, no change of direction, no sudden movement. I couldn't understand it. Then it disappeared. If I was worried before, I was doubly worried now. I searched every ridge and shadow in sight. Moments turned to minutes. I reloaded and fired again. It was back, closer than before and strangely familiar. Like a grounded parachute, its shape changed with the wind, then rolled, billowed, and floated skyward. I didn't know whether to laugh or to curse.   Never before had a garbage bag given me an adrenalin rush, and when it finally passed me, I put a 22 into it, just out of spite.

The snow returned half way across the Valley Bay. Landmarks smudged, blurred, then erased themselves. I was slipping into a twilight zone. Ghostly shapes melted into the gloom, while others materialized out of it. A tree frozen in transit was mistaken for people, a patch of freeze-burned moss for open water. My mind had drifted from the lake to that of a lunar landscape.

By mid-afternoon, the skies were starched white, but as the sun dropped, the colour returned. The gloom broke, and pockets of vision returned. Then at Charley's Point, the lake telescoped down a border of mountains to a flat horizon. And as the sun set, its surface turned into liquid gold.

I woke before dawn. The stars were still out and the lake a deep, icy blue. Last night's wind had hardened the snow like concrete and fluted it in pointed patterns like ripples on a beach.

I was now walking fifteen miles point to point. Lowlands was just a blimp on a flat horizon, and after two hours it seemed no closer. It was soul-destroying. By all accounts I should have been travelling on a six lane freeway, 'Toronto in rush hour', I'd been told, but nothing was further from the truth. In fact, I had had no human contact since leaving Rigolet. With few distractions, my mind started to tick off pressure ridges passed like so many railway stations. Once spotted, my eyes focused in on the next ridge, familiarized themselves with its shape, then locked it into my route. I refused to think of anything else. I made a game of guessing my arrival time, setting my watch alarm, then gunning it for all I was worth.

By noon, the game was over. All colour was bleached. Shadows disappeared. Snowdrifts and pressure ridges climbed on top of each other, all definition was lost , and the mountain views, so spectacular in morning light, melted into a heat haze of monotony. I was down to my T-shirt. My eskimo tan was getting an arm job, and by mid-afternoon, the first signs of a Newfie blush had appeared.

By 2:00 p.m. I was angling into Lowland Point. I was sunburned. My forehead felt red hot and my skin was stretched to tearing point. I wanted shade and rest, in that order, and was within spitting distance of the shore line when a familiar noise massaged my ear drums.

"Seen any seals?". It was your typical lone ranger out from Rigolet en route to the 'Valley' on a beer run."Good day for walking, m'boy".

Meeting up with a ski-doo was always a good excuse to take a leak and light up a cigarette, and once these customs were out of the way, the meetings would pass on to the next stage. "How far.........?" I'd learned from past encounters with ski-doos that whenever their owners gave information relevant to time and distance, it should first be tripled, divided by two, then added to the original number.   I'd derived this formula through trial and error. In this country, a child is given the keys to a ski-doo when most city children are still trying to conquer the first stages of bicycle balance. Nobody walks these days. Everyone on the coast travels by ski-doo and speed and distance are calculated accordingly. I worked on the principal that a good day's walk is one hour ski-doo time, but even that formula had its margins of error.

The meeting wasn't without its velvet lining. Apparently the brook I was aiming for had a trapper's tilt at its mouth and thirty minutes later I was digging myself into it.

The tilt was your conventional six feet by eight feet built of undressed logs caked with moss, with a roof sloped steeply outwards from a central ridge pole, maybe six feet at its apex and three feet at its eaves. The only light inside came from single pane window above the trap door. The floor was covered with a fresh layer of boughs and a small pile of split juniper wood lay by its tin stove. Soon my toes were curled around the heat and my dried food was coming to life in waves of flavour. It was intoxicating, 5-star perfection and with a ravenous appetite satisfied, I was in heaven.

Just before turning in, a tell-tale flutter made me reach for my gun. It was a ptarmigan. Load... aim... fire. CHRIST!!! Instant pain. The bird disintegrated. and the gun recoil almost tore my shoulder off. Feathers fluttered down from all directions and the snow was stained red. I'd just fired a 1oz slug, good enough to drop a polar bear at one hundred paces. Thank God I didn't have to hunt for my supper.

Dawn brought with it snow squalls, heavy drifting and fierce winds. The lake was one massive
witches' cauldron, just the kind of morning to test a
man's metal. I had been told many stories about the
old trappers-their strength and determination against
all odds, and especially the speed with which they
could cover great distances, impressed me, but
always there was a wifey or girlfriendat the end of the
trail. I took one more look at the lake, turned inside
and then crawled back into my dreams.

By 9:00 a.m. the wind had dropped. I was now
following the lazy curve to Julia Point. The horizon
was constantly changing, but never quite producing
what I wanted to see. It was worse than yesterday. I
expected to see Mulligan's Bay round each corner
and my disappointment increased at every turn.
Even the sun worked against me. The crust weakened in the heat and my feet broke through. Not
enough for snow shoes, but enough to irritate and
before long my feet were like two wet sponges. Then
right out of the blue, it began to snow.

Whoever thought up the term 'MOTHER
NATURE' had at least chosen the right gender. Just
when I was beginning to think I could read the signs,
it turned all my lessons inside out. The weather had
teased and wrong-footed me from day one and once
again was laughing at my amateur forecasting. On
reaching Long Point, I gave up at the first signs of life.
John Montague gave me the keys to his cabin and by
late afternoon, Bernie was horizontal.

I was now on the final lap. Ski-doos flashed past
like random torpedoes and human contact was an
hourly occurrence. At Mulligan's Bay, my nose
picked up the first scent of civilization and when I
made camp for the last time at Sebaskachu Point, its
source could be seen like a fireball in the night sky. I
was less than ten miles from the settlement of North
West River and less than thirty miles from the town of
Goose Bay. For the first time, the end of my walk was

in sight. There would be no more cozy cabins, crystal snow, or savage cold nights. I'd miss the nightly entertainment of ghostly shapes called the Northern Lights and tomorrow would be the last opportunity to set my alarm by a bronze sunrise. Central heating is a poor substitute for a crackling camp fire, and you can't beat eating on an empty stomach after a back-breaking day in the harness. Only yesterday, I was cursing the elements and the end couldn't have come fast enough. Now the thought of finishing depressed me.

Goose Bay was only the half-way point. I would have to find a place to stay for two months until the ice broke up, then it was my plan to continue north by sea kayak to Nain. Hotels were out of the question. I was on a limited budget. Until now I had been little more than a passing road show. "The Walking Man" cometh. Families adopted me, I was a commodity, an instant celebrity who breezed in and out of their lives. In the last three months, it had been an endless succession of hellos and goodbyes. I was little more than a hiccup in community life, like a B movie that only stayed long enough to be enjoyed. This time, it would be different. I wanted a place for two months, a place where I could retreat to and call home. But where? Little did I know then, but that question was answered twelve months before on the streets of Toronto. A chance meeting with a friend of a friend and a scribbled name on a piece of paper: "When you get to Goose Bay, give Joe a call". I still had that piece of paper and, on arrival in North West River, used its numbers on the first telephone I saw.

"Hello, is this Joe Goudie?". Poor old Joe, he didn't stand a chance, and no sooner had he answered than I hit him with everything, from my adventures on the coast to my orphan of travel routine. For five minutes, I wined and dined him with all the heart-tugging stories in my repertoire.

"Okay, Bernie. Call me again when you get into Goose. I'll come and pick you up". Whoopee! I felt like a young kid let off detention. One phone call and half my problems were solved. I was in a celebrating mood. That night I allowed myself the luxury of a 'Bed and Breakfast', a six-pack, and my first banana since Toronto.

My last day was anointed with a snow storm. I had decided at the last minute to take Highway 520 from North West River to Goose Bay, rather than the ski-doo trail via Sandy Point, Rabbit Island and the Churchill River. I was in no mood for side trips and the thought of picking my way across bad ice at the mouth of the Naskaupi River was one worry too many.

It was 10:30 a.m. before I finally jump-started my body and headed over the bridge from North West River to Sheshatshiu. It may have been my last day, but it wouldn't pass without incident.

How many times do you see someone walking by the side of a main road pulling a bright orange sled? A strange sight to say the least. I caught many people off-guard that morning, and by the afternoon, I had become a tourist attraction. One man pulled over, stuck his video camera out and fired off five minutes of silly walks. Three more stopped for autographs, and one lady, camera in hand to frame her child with the 'walking man', took a photo. I also drank two beers, a coke and ate half a fruit cake.

It was Friday, April 11th. I arrived in Goose Bay just as the sun was setting. I was tired but happy. In three months, I had put on eight pounds, covered 800 miles and jumped through every hoop of weather the coast offered. I felt fitter than I'd felt in years and was relaxing in the afterglow of a hard trip finished, when Joe arrived.

Two hours later, I was snoring. I was exhausted with relief, but it was a brandy that landed the knock-out punch. The bed was soft and inviting, and its fresh clean sheets slipped over my body like silk. Unfortunately, my heart was still pumping to the walking beat and my brain to the outdoor clock. The noise of cars activated my alarm bells and street lights stung into my eyes like grains of sand. I couldn't sleep. The buzz of excitement kept on returning and I spent my first night in Goose Bay more awake than asleep.

My gears changed fast. I soon became a couch potato with a fetish for TSN and fresh fruit. I cleaned out the local variety store of bananas, indulged in four hours of videos and filled up the gaps with crisp apples and dark grapes. All went well until supper time on the third day, then the flood gates opened.

For months my stomach had been lined with fatty foods. Now it was under an acid attack. One minute I was eating a pizza, the next doubled-up on the toilet seat.

It didn't take long for the aches and pains of travel to surface. The good life at Joe's had softened me up. With no focus, each ailment was magnified. My thighs constantly throbbed and both ankles made strange cracking noises. My blood-shot eyes gave me the appearance of an airhead on drugs and my sore nose looked like a cancerous growth. Idleness led to imaginary diseases. I needed to fill the days, start looking for a more permanent home. The day I went ice-fishing to Mud Lake was the day the problem was solved.

After a hard day on the trail you couldn't beat the Northern Lights for free entertainment.

Crossing Partridge Bay en route to Black Tickle

Welcome to Labrador
Minus 32 Deg. C.
My start - off point, Red Bay.

A pyramid of driftwood, Cartwright
A common sight on the coast

Looking towards Domino Run from Spotted Islands

View of Spotted Islands from the top of Peter's Hill

I always gave pressure ridges a wide birth.
They looked like mini volcanoes of ice and
just as dangerous

Easter Brook Cabin near Lodge Bay,
built adjacent to the Snowmobile Trail over the Barrens,
it acts as an Emergency Shelter

Red Bay, Emergency Snowmobile Trail Shelter
Thawing out after my first days walk

Trapper's Tilt, Lake Melville

(above & below)
Dig - out time after the blizzard in Black Tickle

The old faithful wood fired 'Ensign' stove
Norman's Bay

Snowmobile Trail Groomer, Charlottetown

Dog sled, Port Hope Simpson

Ski - Doo & Komatik near Lodge Bay
Snowmobiles have the same droning noise a motor bike has minus a
muffler, and at full throttle a pack of them could be mistaken for the
"Indy 500" on race day.

Two laned groomed snowmobile trail between Charlottetown and
Norman's Bay

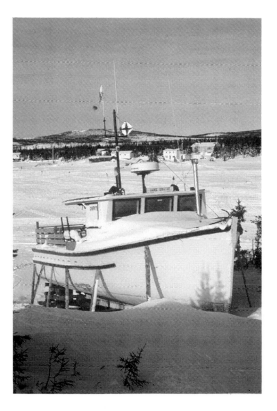

Winter storage, Lodge Bay

Tent City, Mud Lake
Bernie's new home

Drying Smelt

Heat wave...!
Only minus 14 Deg C.

Putting up a tent when it is minus 30 Deg. C. was like asking a surgeon to operate with boxing gloves on

...but once up, you couldn't beat the sight and sound of a roaring fire, your first cuppa tea or the thought of a plate full of steaming beans

Bernie taking a side trip up the Kenamu River
cold was never a problem when walking - sweating was

With no visable
snowmobile tracks to
follow trail markers
were my only life - line.
They came in all
shapes and sizes;
Pyramids of sticks,
painted boulders, wood
nailed to trees, old gas
tanks strung from
branches and even
beer cans

Trying out my new kayak on the Churchill River
For a guy with no experience of sea kayaking, I sure looked
confident that day.

I was now used to psychoanalyzing myself by a weather forecaster,s
report. Rained in - depression; strong northeasterlies - grounded;
sunny and clear - life couldn't be better. Today it was a touch of
sunny with cloudy periods - no problemo

An eerie graveyard of ice caused by strong easterly winds
View from Cape Rouge to Cape Harrison

Grounded iceberg near Windy Tickle
The comparison of icebergs and skyscrapers is no idol observation.
Like the one above some were gothic and austere with sharp
perpindicular lines pointing skywards while others were squat with
smooth sculptured surfaces

Photo: Newfoundland and Labrador Tourism

This Humpback Whale was too close for comfort

Maybe it was a case of safety in numbers or maybe they'd never been hunted before by a bright yellow kayak. Harp seals were fearless. They dotted the offshore ice like freckles, popping up here and there all sad - eyed like those of a wet puppy dog.

Photo: Maynard Brown

The Tavener docking at Rigolet wharf
To some the boat's decks were as familiar as home, yet for others
they could be under the influence of weather and the dreaded 'gravol
pill' as bleak as prisons

Photo: Tim Borlase

Rigolet has its narrows; Makkovik is second left past Cape
Strawberry and Postville has only one entrance down Kaipoko Bay,
but searching for Hopedale's red and white radio antenna through a
maze of islands proved a major headache

Bakeapples are not so much a unique taste as a journey. Picked locally, their golden suntans set them apart. Some Newfies call them liquid gold and if given the choice would gladly adopt them as local currency

Who said black bears can't climb trees

Photo: Mick Emmens

Whow! What a pair of legs...after two years in Labrador it was time
to return home to Toronto via the Trans - Labrador Highway

Photo: Brad Keats

Nine months in the fast lane was enough. By June of '94 I had
thrown in the towel, packed my bags, bought a new kayak and
headed east down the St.Lawrence back to Labrador...but that's
another story

Chapter 13
HalfWay House called Mud Lake

SEVEN MILES DOWN STREAM ON THE Churchill River, and still influenced by tidal waters, Mud Lake is located on the banks of a small channel. It was love at first sight. It had everything: a small convenience store, a friendly "Beautiful day for walking, boy" post mistress called Clara, but most of all it was its location on the opposite side of the river from Goose Bay. That meant people traffic would be cut down to the most adventurous and with no connecting bridge or village roads, the only way to get across would be by ski-doo in winter and speed boat in summer. Peace and quiet and a roof over my head, what else could I ask for? Two days later I exchanged Joe's modern lifestyle for a rustic one room log cabin, and by week's end I had slipped from an oddity to be stared at to being part of the scenery. Invites for supper came thick and fast, caribou meat and trout appeared at my doorstep and I had no problem getting help for wood collection or borrowing a chain saw to cut it up.

Spring was in overdrive. The sun now carried with it the property of heat, and my sunglasses became an essential part of outdoor life. The ice was great to travel on and ski-doos were out in force. Labrador had woken up to its favourite pastime, ice fishing, and that meant ice chisels, scoops, augers and of course your favourite hook and line. The trout were moving and smelts were being hooked by the dozen.

Colour finally returned to the north. Willows were budding, ferns forced their way up daily and ground moss was exchanging its deep brown winter coat for one of lush green. A week before, the snow was whiter than white, now the full weight of a changing

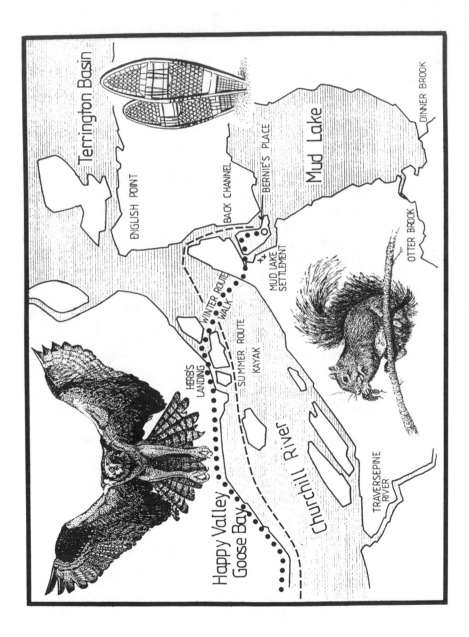

season had forced up six months of fallen garbage. Man-made noises had dropped to an all-time low. Ski-doos were disappearing fast. The snow trails were all gone and the frozen river paths were more slush than ice. The mighty River Churchill was starting to show signs of break-up. Huge cracks appeared and large ponds of black ice were a constant reminder of rapid thawing. Brooks chuckled with the noise of open water and snow retreated wherever the sun poured down its rays. Any day now, the back channel would open. In recent days, the ice had gone from being snow-covered, to crystal blue and then to dangerously weakened, air bubble-filled, dirty white.

Then it happened. A sonic boom, hours of tearing and the channel was free. In eight hours, my back garden turned into a huge mirror and by the end of the day, the snow-capped Mealey Mountains were reflected in its waters. Sadly it didn't last long. Winter did a U-turn. Overnight temperatures plummeted by 40 degrees. A wicked arctic high tore in from Ungava and, once again, new frost locked away the water like a steel door. Occasionally, the silence was broken by the tearing noises of thin ice and the gurgle of rushing water. The channel's stomach was complaining under the strain of a rising tide. Inevitably, it peaked, dropped, and left the ice high and dry.

BOOM..BOOM..BOOM..PANG..PANG..PANG..

Echoes and cracks criss-crossed the channel and beyond. Space-age star wars with laser guns played out their sound tracks as cracks opened, closed, then shattered like glass. For two days the frost held firm, then once again temperatures rose, ice cracked and the water broke free.

After so many months of lifeless skies, birds exploded onto the scene. First to touch down were the black ducks, then came the canvas backs, loons, gozzards, and lastly a company of divers. A pair of osprey chose to nest behind my camp while a pair of jays declared war on my scraps. Later I was joined inside by a pair of squirrels and soon whatever wasn't nailed down, screwed in or bagged out of reach, became shared property. It was that time of the year; hormones were starting to itch and courting was in the air. Quarrels became a daily occurrence. High-pitched squeaks and throaty ticks became the norm. My neighbourhood squirrels were heading for the stew pot, then an owl appeared and silence returned.

Outside, the channel turned into a bustling metropolis. Real estate was at a premium; ducks took over the broader waters, divers the willows, and osprey the rest. Patience was the name of their game and catching the right air current the influence that directed bird to fish. I counted six lazy spirals one morning: osprey were at play, but once locked into a trout, they were all action. Wings folded, they looked like guided missiles and would drop vertically into the water. After so many months of silence, to hear the whine of ducks in the air, the splash of an osprey striking water or the haunting cry of a loon, was exhilarating. The air waves were full of noises and when one evening a huge male moose made a cameo appearance it was a dream come true.

You can have too much of a good thing. After three months of eating game meat it was hard to view my new feathered friends without sometimes picturing them on my plate. I wasn't the only one. Boats were being cleaned, engines tuned and when I was woken at 6:00p.m. to the sound of gunfire, I knew that the spring duck hunt had officially started. Overnight, I exchanged the sound of a pristine wilderness for that of DESERT STORM. I couldn't even go for a piss without first looking in both directions. Every morning twelve gauges lay in wait. I could set my alarm clock by them and every evening the night sky echoed with their repeated volleys.

To add colour and confusion to the scene, Mud Lake's population doubled. A band of Innu from Sheshatshiu moved in. Tents sprouted up like mushrooms after rain and soon their location had the unmistakable signature of a blue haze above them. The Neskapi Indian was acting on his traditional rite, the 'spring hunt', and before long they were regular visitors.

My cabin quickly turned into a revolving door. Water was always on the boil and my tin of tobacco didn't know the word closed. It became the daily meeting place for the 'gumly' smile, the 'stretched at birth' and those with deep gravel tones that only a 'two pack a day' man can achieve. The evenings were full of tall stories and the only house rule was that a colourful lie was better than a dull truth. I was among kindred spirits and as such made instant contact.

It was now the end of May. The sun woke me before 5:00a.m. and didn't drop till after 9:00p.m. The snow was rapidly melting and the flies were just hatching. The days were endless, but mine had geared down. The ducks had nearly all moved on and so had the hunters. Peace was returning. It was time for a new adventure and I didn't have far to travel for the experience.

The Churchill River was breaking up. I didn't want to miss a minute of it and, wanting to get up close, borrowed a canoe.

The day started innocently enough. I tucked in behind Smoke Island, watched and waited. The tide was changing and as the currents changed the ice pans wheeled with it. Tearing noises were coming from the bank and cracks and booms from every direction. The river was dancing with the debris of last years freeze-up. I watched in awe as two huge slabs of ice kissed, crunched in embrace, then rose in slow motion before diving back into the river. Bushes entombed in ice flowed by and huge trees set adrift by the spring tides rolled by dangerously close. Up stream break-up was in full swing. From a distance the once smooth surface now looked like a thousand panes of broken glass. I knew it was dangerous, but I wanted a closer look. The waters were swollen and eddies stronger than anticipated. I was too far back in the canoe when the bow turned. I couldn't hold it. Ice flows were everywhere. I back paddled, gained some space, turned and headed for shore. Another ice flow, another back paddle. I was slipping further into the hole. It was hit and miss, then a gap appeared. I was back in open water. Then the inevitable happened. I struck ice. Suddenly, the bank disappeared, my view arced and water came in. The canoe was sucked down, held, then released as if from an elastic band. The whole incident lasted seconds, but its adrenalin rush hung on.

On the way back I ran into an ice jam. The tide was running and large ice flows had knitted tightly together, blocking the back channel and my progress home. It was now dusk and difficult to see where the dark pools of water began and the black ice ended. My decision to hop out and pull the canoe over the ice wasn't taken lightly, but when the adrenalin is flowing anything seems possible. Just the other day I had experienced exactly the same problem. On that occasion it was follow my leader. I relied on a friend and local knowledge to see me across but this time I was on my own. It was sink or swim. For five glorious minutes I had the adventure of a lifetime. I picked my way across one ice flow after another, checking ice surfaces with the paddle while never letting go of the canoe with my free hand. Knuckles went white and I could hear nerves jangling against each other. For five minutes I rubbed up against my own fear and by the time I made open water my face was creased with its tension. Ten minutes later, I was home. My fears fell back to a whisper and once more colour returned to my cheeks. I had been bitten by the incident, but far from deterring my thirst for the kayak trip ahead, it only enhanced it.

For two weeks, I argued the merits of either flying in my kayak tomorrow, or waiting till a questionable ice break-up in June. My kayak was in St. John's awaiting a decision. On one side of the ledger, flying it in would cost an added four hundred and fifty dollars, but on the other side it would give me some breathing space. The coastal ferry service from Lewisport, Nfld. to Goose Bay, Labrador wasn't expected to start until mid-June. I could check equipment, get in some practice, but most importantly I could relax in the knowledge it was here. That morning I booked the kayak on LabAir's freight service.

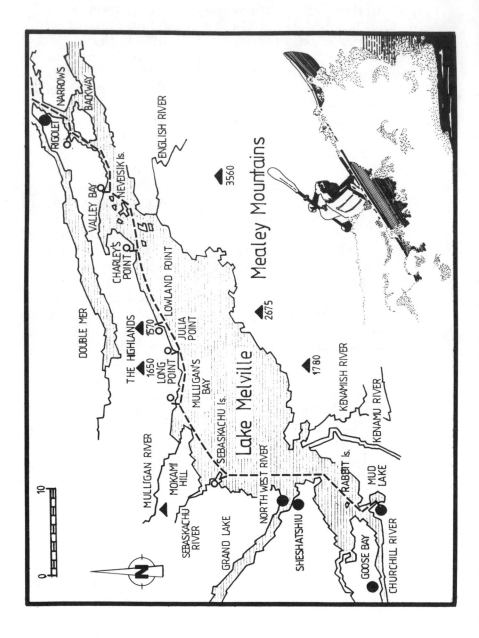

Chapter 14
Gates of Hell

ENTHUSIASM IS ONE THING, KNOWLEDGE another. What I knew about sea kayaking you could fit on the back of a postage stamp. I had only spent six hours in a kayak before and two of those were practicing stroke techniques in the calm waters of a sheltered harbour. I had never tried or being taught the Eskimo roll, and the only lesson I learned from executing an emergency re-entry was not to get wet in the first place. My plan was to have a love affair with the coastline, hug it, sleep with it and never buck its weather. I didn't care if I had to walk miles of coastline, portage every Cape, or skip every day except the breathless ones. The last thing I wanted was to become a rescue case and although long ago I gave in to the fact that I wouldn't live to a ripe old age, I had no intention of cashing in my chips in the very near future.

I decided a couple of lessons in the Eskimo roll wouldn't go amiss. I booked my kayak into the Goose Bay Recreation Centre, obtained permission from its director to use it in the pool, then spent two afternoons under his supervision. If anyone tells you it's easy roll a kayak, they're bullshitting. I never completed a single roll. I did, however, learn to appreciate life underwater, acquire a taste for chlorine and realize why the float was invented.

Back home in Mud Lake, my brilliant yellow kayak became a daily sight. I was like a young kid with a new toy and I played with it until I grew blisters. Every night I packed and unpacked equipment until I forgot the reason why I started.

Each morning I woke to a floor arrangement of water proof bags, positioned in the order they would take in my kayak. There were three piles. The bow contained toiletries, repair kits and one pair of dry clothes. For easy access, between my legs in the cockpit and suitably waterproofed, I would squeeze in the sleeping bag and shotgun. The largest pile went into the stern hatch. It contained the bulk of my clothes, three weeks' supply of dehydrated food, cooking utensils and stove. Stability was a major priority and I was reluctant to store anything in the deck rigging but in the end that was the only place I could find to store the tent.

I could now pack and unpack blindfolded. Early glitches had been ironed out. My stroke had found a rhythm and my seat, so uncomfortable at first, was now adjusted to my liking. I had replaced my rudder cables, and they now worked like a dream. Early heat rashes caused by my skin-tight wet suit had vanished and now felt like a second skin. I had bought over twenty 1: 50,000 scale maps and now knew the location of every rock, tickle and point to be rounded. They were all covered with notes, 'intended routes on calm days', 'alternates' and 'escape routes in case of bad weather'. Local knowledge had come up trumps and my address book was filled with contact names in every settlement up the coast. I was ready.

By mid-June, the first boats arrived in Goose Bay. The ice in Lake Melville had cleared and the only obstacle holding me back was saying my goodbyes.

I've lost count of goodbyes made over the years, but it hasn't made them any easier. Mud Lake had got under my skin. It had turned into much more than a layover between chapters. I'd made friends, good friends. Now I had to turn my back on them. When travelling through a new experience, I can't afford the luxury of looking over my shoulder. I've worked out my own formula. The more a parting means, the more casual it is, and if I could have slipped out unnoticed I would have. But it wasn't to be.

One always wants to go an see and know, but actually to be going - that is something else. My last night in Mud Lake I could hardly sleep with excitement. I must have capsized twice, fast-forwarded those pesky polar bears and been chased from sleep at least once by killer whales. I awoke in the morning to another hungry animal, a television crew. My trip up the coast was news; Bernie was now public property. Over the years I had exchanged the mantle of 'mad cap' adventurer to that of 'travel writer'. I now needed the media as much as they needed me.

The morning was staged and recorded, then broadcasted on "Here and Now" as a news item. It was official. Bernie was on his way to Nain.

For the first time since starting this trip, I was beginning to ask the question, why? WHY LABRADOR?

Born in England, I emigrated to Canada in the early 70's and have been travelling ever since, but usually in warmer climates. I've tasted the American Dream, got under the surface of Asia, and have been bitten by the darker sides of Africa. In the process, I've seen the power of hurricanes, woken up to a volcanic eruption, and even lived through a bloody civil war in Uganda. A man who has experienced all this and logged 30,000 miles cycling around the world on his own doesn't have to prove himself to anyone. But here I am nine days into my kayaking trip and I've not even reached my first port of call, Rigolet. I was overdue, suffering hypothermia and beginning to doubt my own sanity.

My first day out from Mud Lake ended quickly. I only made Rabbit Island. I didn't plan it that way, my stomach did. Somehow I managed to stretch a ten minute snack into a thirty minute orgy. Baked apple squares, fruit cake, chocolate chip cookies, I ate them all and by 5:00 p.m. I was asleep.

The next day was glass calm. I made good mileage to Sebaskachu, but from there on, things got serious.

Crossing Mulligan's Bay, I got caught in a sudden squall. Within minutes, calm waters boiled. Spray shot past like bullets. Wind and current were in conflict and waves clapping in all directions. I felt like a ping-pong ball in a table tennis match.

"You're stupid, you've never even kayaked before". I remembered those words. Comments like that came from people who didn't know me; people who did offered only encouragement. My best advice came from a lady who had paddled the Pacific.

"It's all in your hips and in your head", she said. "Don't fight the waves, just let them go under you. Balance, that's the key, and if things get desperate, concentrate on the point you are aiming for and don't get sucked into the waves. If you think you're going to capsize, you will".

The lady was full of common sense. She hadn't offered books, told me to research or even buy sophisticated equipment. Maybe her advice wasn't for everyone, but it sure struck a chord with me.

The squall didn't last long, but was tiring. Fear didn't enter into the equation. It wasn't my nerves, it was my body. I couldn't sit up straight without wincing and my arms, having pumped like wind mills, were played out. It was game, set and match. The beach couldn't come fast enough, shortly followed by food, sleeping bag and the blissful void called sleep.

Outside, the early evening weather went from bad to worse. A storm was brewing. By early evening, the sun had gone. A brassy glare took the place of clear daylight. Even the air that swept down the lake was hot and held little refreshment. Colours had drained from the water, the Mealies blurred and the white and brown clouds brooded. Nothing prospered but the flies. It was the calm before the storm. Mosquitoes were on an eating frenzy and flies wedded in lust. The atmosphere was like a hot knife on butter and just as sticky. Then, without, warning marbles of rain dropped. At first, a scattered one hit the tent; ping, my pot was hit. Pat...pat, then the heavens opened. It rained all night.

I fared no better next day past Julia Point. My body hadn't recovered from Mulligan's and the weather had turned up a notch. The sky was a checkered quilt of black and white and the wind now came directly out of the east. Rain gave way to flurries, then to rain again. My arms were going through the motions but my hands, even with wool gloves on and protected in 'poggie' paddle covers, had lost nearly all sense of touch. The sting of wind chill crept from finger tip to knuckle and now enveloped my hand like a vice. The pain, acute in the morning, had dulled to a throbbing ache by noon. It wore away at my senses and when it turned to pins and needles, I threw in the towel and called it a day at Lowland Point.

I woke to a torrential downpour. It came in dark swirling curtains, whiplashing my face and making the sea roar. I was now paddling in a full blown storm, but for all the conditions, I felt great. For starters, I owned the lake. I hadn't seen or heard anything since Sebaskachu, but more importantly, I was now adjusting to my new home. I didn't twist and twitch in my seat anymore. Foam rubber pads cushioned my rear and an inflatable one my back. Knee pads allowed me the luxury of comfort. I could now jam them into the cockpit's side without soreness. It's surprising how your body adapts to new positions and muscles to new work, but one bodily function just wouldn't play the game.

There are certain questions you never ask in polite conversation, certain issues that never get into print. It was so simple, it never entered my head. It's not that I'm a prude, but how do you set the mood to ask the question: 'Where do you piss?' It's not that I have a problem with my 'rod'. It's adequate, does the job and is toilet trained, at least I thought it was. Mind over matter I'm told. Well, it might work for the disciples of Indian mystics, but it didn't for me. Every time my brain said 'Head for shore', my bowels said 'Hurry up'. I couldn't paddle fast enough. It got so bad that even the thought of turning for shore set off a chain reaction and believe me, when the flood gates open it's all down hill. I soon gave up the battle and by Lowlands, I took to adding my ablutions to the cockpit and my pollutants, via a sponge, to the sea.

The weather really turned ugly at Charley's Point. For the last three days, strong winds from the east had geared down my progress to a crawl and now it was blowing a gale. I know I shouldn't have tried it, but I wanted to experience extreme conditions before I got onto the open sea. Any other reason would have been crazy.

At first I drifted out from Point to mid-channel to gain the tide, but the winds blew me backwards. Sixty minutes later, I was back where I started. I was now so close to the cliffs I could almost touch them. Progress was painfully slow; tidal whirlpools and strong back eddies meant every yard gained was a battle.

It took me two hours to cover three miles. Rain cut like pins into my face and back swells had the waves clapping and cresting all over the place. Everywhere the surface was streaked with foam. I still hadn't struck a rhythm with my paddle stroke, and when fatigue hit, it came quickly. I hadn't got the strength to search out a good camp site or the sense to choose the right wave. I took the first opportunity for both, scraped, crunched and aged ten years, but found a foothold on a blade of greenery. That night I slept in one cove while my kayak lay high and dry beached on rocks in another. There just wasn't enough room for both of us.

One battle doesn't end a war, but yesterday's experience catapulted my confidence through the roof. I was now ready for open water. My original plan was to hug the shoal waters round Valley Bay, but no sooner had the sun peaked over the Mealy Mountains than I set course for Neveisik Islands. By early afternoon I was back on firm ground. I'd let go of the land, crossed open water and won the battle of nerves. I was now ready for the 'Narrows'.

You won't find the name 'Gates of Hell' on any nautical map, but to the more informed officiandos of paddle, that's what the Narrows should be called. It's one thing to see it from land and another to dip your toes into its waters. Fifteen miles in length and bordered by steep hills, it cuts a dangerous path no matter what the weather. There are no light, joyful colours on its waters. The Narrows is the kind of place that gives life to the term gloom and doom. I dreaded it, but the closer I got the more excited I became. The scene was set: dark angry clouds, spitting rain and a howling wind. Timing was everything. The tide influences everything from fish to speedboats to passenger ships. You don't buck two hundred million gallons of water when gravity releases it.

Everything went wrong that day. First I misjudged the tide. I had camped at Big Pot Cove and while I watched the tide rise, unknowingly two miles away in the Narrows, it was roaring out. If that wasn't enough, the 'Northern Ranger'(coastal ferry boat) was bearing down in my direction.

I found the current in mid-channel. I was on automatic. The strong current gave the illusion of moving quickly, but as a tree stump drifted past my eyes focused on the shore. Holy Shit! Tide rips - cross currents - whirlpools. My clay foot of inexperience was showing. I was going backwards, no, sideways. Actually, I wasn't going anywhere. My paddle was pushing off against fresh air. I was bobbing about in a pool of bubbles like a rudderless cork, then suddenly the current came back, my paddle bit and I was off again.

Ten minutes later I was out of control again. The incoming sea tide was now rushing full tilt over outgoing lake water. Long sheets of counterflow ripped the surface to shreds. I wasn't in the mood for natural wonders. The whole scene was foreign and I couldn't get out fast enough.

Suddenly a seal popped up. There's a time and a place, but not when you're trying to execute a 90 deg. turn away from an onrushing rock. Too late. I struck the rock, broadsided the current and had it not been for the wind would have taken an early bath. I now had my nose in the Narrows, but little else. For sixty minutes I had dashed from one eddy to another. Not my kind of fun and when I finally turned the corner into Caravalla Cove, Doug Adams' cabin beckoned.

For the first time in nine days I had the opportunity to dry out. I didn't think time would ever pass until I warmed up, but it did. The stove was cooking, and every hook and rafter had a guest drying on it. I was surrounded by steam. From tent to spare underwear, everything was either wet or damp. Even my body. Getting wet in the morning was a daily occurrence and constant rain meant staying wet all day. My only reliable towel was baby powder, which I had used nightly. I had bought a 700 gram container before leaving and now it was almost empty.

The storm had taken its toll. My body's old pink healthiness had paled. Skin was starting to crack and cuts to pus. My wrist had swollen and the slightest movement felt like sandpaper on glass. My fingers, wet and cold from six days of continual rain, had swollen like sausages. Just looking at myself in the mirror was depressing; eyes sunk, hair knotted, and lips lined and wrinkled like an old man. But, and it was a big but, it couldn't get any worse. Tomorrow Rigolet was a certainty. I'd walk it if I had to and I held onto the thought all night.

It was now day ten and Rigolet was in sight. For

the last seven days, I had been paddling down the throat of an easterly wind with 'GALE WARNINGS' in effect up and down the coast. I was cold, wet, and very tired. That question, why Labrador? still hung around my neck. My back ached, my arms felt like lead weights and my legs were torn with cramps. Rigolet was now rushing towards me and I could see a group of on-lookers down in the harbour.

I arrived in Rigolet at 2:00 pm. on July 3rd. Smiles went unnoticed, shouts unacknowledged. Other things were on my mind. I was heading for the Grenfell Mission and wild horses couldn't drag me from my course. "Why Labrador?" was about to be answered.

"Linda, could I have a bath?"

Ten minutes later all my aches and pains were dissolving in hot water. The answer: HOSPITALITY.

Life on the coast is a catalogue of changing silhouettes. You learn from an early age to put names to shapes, and sounds of engines are the calling cards that make one reach for the binoculars. It's an age-old tradition to take time out and visit the wharf when a ship docks. The more remote the community, the bigger the greeting. It begs the question, "What's the attraction?".

Preplanned entertainment on the coast is a rarity. You can't go window shopping, catch a movie, or go to a ball game. Self-reliance is a Labradorian's common backbone. You play cards at home, bingo by radio and outdoor recreation is definitely of the pick-up variety, so when an event can be scheduled it turns into a community affair.

Outside of LabAir, Marine Atlantic has cornered the market on coastal transportation. From Red Bay to Nain, the 'Northern Ranger' and 'Tavener' have become regular items on the Labrador landscape. They're no 'Love Boat,' but what these floating hotels lack in speed and comfort they more than make up for in the personal touch. Rich in history, sea travel is still the transport of choice for the young at heart and the adventurous of spirit.

Every spring, Labrador is invaded by new dialects. After seven months of isolation, new faces must have come like a breath of fresh air. Who could blame heads for turning? Romantic place names like Come-by-Chance, Hearts Desire, Savage Cove and Harbour Deep must have had a strong pull on youthful imaginations and I bet there was more than just a little stowaway in all of them. That was yesterday. Today the fisheries are in decline. Tourism is rapidly filling the empty seats and Newfie accents are being replaced by foreign languages. The excitement of seeing a distant cousin from Newfoundland may be fading fast, but the lure of things different remains. Whatever the attraction, there was no doubting the majority of youthful faces at the wharf. From the moment the Tavener's bow appeared down Hamilton Inlet, to the first sounds of its signal horn, its presence attracted bodies like a magnet.

The Tavener docked in organised confusion and, with no uniformed administrators, ticket offices or queues to contend with, help was of the back-to-basic variety. The first rope to hit the wharf lost itself to a swarm of children, while the second, thrown with pin-point accuracy, traced its way like a major league curve ball into the hands of a nimble retiree. By the time the gang-plank hit the wharf it was anyone's guess who were the paying customers. Bodies, like the crates and boxes of their owners, were coming and going in all directions, but I didn't hear one voice of complaint. By now the children had the run of the decks. Never smothered in regulations, they could explore and meet with friends for just the time it took for passengers and freight to be brought aboard and not a minute longer. Then it would be back home with a battery of new stories until the next time. Locals used this ferry service like we use a city bus. Weekly stopovers are as normal to them as our nightly visits to family and friends. You can't exactly set your watch by their schedule, but that was half the fun. They could be storm-bound for days, and I never heard of them turning away late arrivals or failing to stop at sea to pick up passengers chasing on speed boats.   Four times I've travelled on the service between Port-aux-Basque and North Sydney and once between Red Bay and Lewisporte. Rough and ready, yes, but they were never boring. Bumps in the night, laughter and guitar music were their nightly rhythms and it was not unusual to trip over embraces locked in sleep or to be woken by somebody else's natural alarm clock.They have a community atmosphere, where you either blend in or go sleepless To some the boats decks are as familiar as home; for others they can be under the influence of weather and the dreaded 'gravol pill', as bleak as prisons. Partners could be seduced, courtships cemented, and discussions and gossip could and often did stretch through the night. In short, to travel by Marine Atlantic wasn't so much a trip as an experience and the day after it left, so did Bernie.

Chapter 15
Sea at Last

IKEPT HAVING IMAGES OF HUGE SEA SWELLS and a bi-line on the back page, 'Missing at sea'. I certainly wasn't suffering from over-confidence, but the knot in my stomach was from excitement not fear.

Rigolet marked the end of sheltered waterways. Ahead Hamilton Inlet's corridor tapered down into a blue haze. I was all pumped up. My reasons for coming were just around the corner in the open sea. Salt was in the air and the smell of rotting seaweed triggered childhood memories of sandcastles, flying surf and the sound of gulls.

I timed my departure to perfection. I left in the grip of an ebb tide. The water was flowing at an incredible speed and my kayak felt like a toy in a bath tub with the plug pulled out. All I had to do was sit back, enjoy the view and operate the rudder. The sky was clear and it wasn't raining. I couldn't ask for a better start. It was July 6th. Summer had finally made its presence felt and to top it off, the long-range weather forecast called for more of the same. A raw breeze fought the tide that morning and brought life to the water and apart from a small group of terns hovering overhead, I had the Narrows to myself.

At Double Mer Point, I ran into two converging flows. For thirty minutes my pace went into over-drive, but once past Ticoralak Head the current released its grip and by Big Island I was out of the fast-flowing Narrows and into the subdued throat tides of Hamilton Inlet. I had covered over ten miles in less than ninety minutes without so much as break-ing sweat. I was actually enjoying myself for once.

By noon the wind had died.The surface was glass-calm and there wasn't a sound to be heard. Then sud-

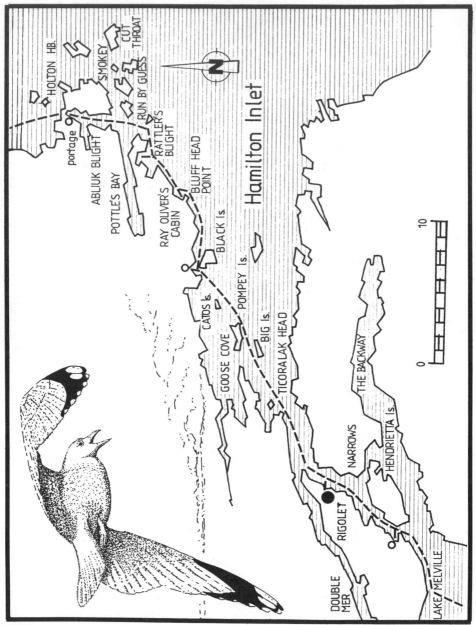

denly the sea burst into life; birds on the wing; one
flock after another; clouds of noise that came from
nowhere. Like mini-volcanoes they spewed up, dispersed , converged, then strung out in all directions.
A flock of red-footed guillemots, streamlined beak to
tail, swung round in my direction like a whiplash
before curving low over the water like a Chinese
paper dragon. Yet another formation appeared, this
time white-tipped male ider ducks. They passed like
bullets and in the process filled my ears with the beating whine of a hundred wings. Then it was the turn
of the diver ducks.   Two flocks criss-crossed each
other as if in aerial combat. Twice they circled my
kayak, splitting on approach, reuniting downstream.
They flew so close that I could have batted them out
of the air.

Shortly before Pompey Island I paddled into a
group of terns in a full-scale eating frenzy. I was now
surrounded by the stereophonic sound of birds dive-
bombing after caplin and by the time the show ended
it was mid-afternoon and time for my first brew-up.

Over the years I have gained a healthy respect for
the mosquito. I work on the principal of live and let
live. I don't mind donating blood for a good cause,
but I draw the line when its user goes for the jugular.
I was only beached for thirty minutes, but I swear
every blood sucker within a mile smelled me coming.
Unlike many people I'm not allergic to bites. It's not
their appetite that gets to me, it's the bloody whining
noise they make while hovering around searching for
decent landing sites. I have more than your average
body hair. They have a hard time landing on my
arms and my neck is covered under a mass of knots
and split ends that is almost impregnable. They can
bite my ears all day and if they can put up with my
face more power to them. So what am I complaining
about? My toilet arrangements. From day one, I had
taken to wearing a full-length wet suit - great against
the cold but awkward when nature asked you to drop
your pants. No sooner had I unzipped, peeled off

and squatted, than my bum was peppered like a pin cushion. You can't hurry nature and you can't call a truce either. The experience changed my routine. There would be no more shoreline brew-ups. In future my coffee breaks would be taken at sea. From now on I would use my thermos, and as for bowel movements, it would be a case of mind over matter.

From Pompey, I took the more direct route via Catos Island to Black Island. The tide was out and the shoreline passage had turned into a mine-field of exposed rocks. It was a judgement call. Six miles of open water with only a barren rock for shelter in case of a storm. Sounds worse than it looked. The sky was clear and there wasn't a hint of swell. I was still miles from the Atlantic's influence. Not exactly life threatening, but still it was a decision.

Weeks before, I had gone over my planned route to Nain with Steve Tooktoshina. Steve is a fisherman with years of experience under his belt. He knew the coastline like the back of his hand. A friend of a friend, his name had been passed down through the chain of contacts I made in Mud Lake. Between us, we covered every inch of coast from Rigolet to Makkovik and by the end of the day my maps had turned into a dictionary of local knowledge. Notes covered everything from cloud formations to uncharted havens of shelter. Escape routes were penciled in against rough weather and direct passages for calm. We covered the alphabet of shoal and reef water, looked into short cuts and island hopping, and made crosses against every known fishing cabin on the coast. Notations from 'go for it on calm day's' to bad, carn't beach in any weather' dotted the maps. Whenever possible, inside passages were counselled and coast-hugging became the order of the day. His bubbly, no-nonsense nature swept me along and his stamp of approval, 'If you take your time and you'll have no problem', was just the tonic my tattered confidence craved. I've never been one to limit myself to other peoples' ideas, but there's a fine line between a healthy risk and a fool hardy death wish, and he left me with no doubt on which side he thought I stood.

It's nice to gun it at the end of the day, empty your batteries and race yourself to the shore. Pain can translate into a glorious sense of achievement when gauged against distance covered, and being hungry and tired only makes one's appetite that much greater. I covered the distance between Pompey and Black Island in a little over two hours, then spent the next two searching for a suitable campsite. Water and driftwood weren't the problem; shelter was. Coastal woodlands are a poor relative to their inland giants. Trees once in abundance around Lake Melville's shoreline had had their tops shaved off and had dwindled back to the base of hills and ravines. What remained above the shoreline looked stunted and deformed in comparison. In just one day the scenery had changed from lush green to pale brown and the vegetation was certain to become scarcer and shorter the further north I went.

Once decided, it took me less than thirty minutes to beach, unpack, erect the tent and light a fire. My winter experience had honed my camping skills and the ten days spent on Lake Melville had given me the time to iron out my beaching technique. When routine becomes second nature you don't have to think and before the sun had sunk below the foothills I was replaying the day's events, tucked up and cushioned in down, drifting through waters in another world.

I set off the following morning into a stiff breeze and no sooner had I slipped out of from behind Black Island than I found myself paddling in a sea swell. I was now hanging onto the coastline like a tightrope walker. Hamilton Inlet had opened into an endless horizon. Just looking at it made me dizzy. One slip now and it would be goodbye Bernie. With the exception of a few natural harbours, the shoreline ahead to Pottle's Bay was a ragged, reef-infested wall of rock. It was a picture that begged a video. Rock and grass, cliffs, headlands, long edges, sharp horizons and the ever present glint of ice. Put to music, the scenes would have looked more like a dream than real life, but when you opened your ears to the pounding surf you knew it wasn't a fairy tale.

Only a few years ago, the names Smokey and Cut Throat meant fish, jobs and boats. But the cod have long since disappeared and fishermen are now on the endangered species list. When planning this trip I had banked on their contact. I had even arranged for a food pick-up at the government store on Smokey, but it was closed, so when I heard a speed boat rounding Bluff Head Point I made for the first signs of life.

"Don't bother with your boots boy, you're in a fish cabin now." I found Ray Oliver tending his gill nets. The salmon were running and he'd taken time out from his permanent job in Goose Bay to follow in his father's footsteps. In meeting Ray I'd unknowingly paddled into a rich vein of contacts. The cod moratorium may have stripped the coastal waters of fishing boats but the salmon and arctic char brought with them their own breed of harvestors.

I first heard the term 'fish cabin' in Mary's Harbour. For the short cod season these cabins turned into second homes and whole families moved lock, stock and barrel to be near the fishing grounds. It never occurred to me that the same culture would follow the salmon and char season.

I gate-crashed the Olivers' like a human hurricane. The children were still in bed, but as soon as my strange dialect hit the airwaves they were up and nibbling around our conversation like a pack of tail wagging husky dogs.

Children are children wherever you go, but there is something special about the coastal urchins of Labrador. The further north you go, the more isolated and the more independent they become. Summer time means no school and, with little television to dull their edges, a time for creative entertainment. Their inquisitive minds may just as likely find their

way to their fathers' gill nets as their boundless energy will find outlets kicking a soccer ball on a postal
stamp of ground, surrounded by rocks. Isolation can
either break a young spirit like a twig or forge it into
steel. With few pre-planned events, reliance on your
brothers and sisters is in bred from an early age and
life skills are worn like a second skin. I stayed at the
Olivers' just long enough to fill my belly with salmon,
take in some local knowledge and answer a battery of
youthful questions.

I was now following a curtain of rocky coast, the
end of which, jutting out below Stag Hill like a sentry
on guard duty, was the dangerous Point of Bar. The
tide was half out and with the exception of a few
exposed rocks the surface looked calm and safe. I
should have given the shoal water a wider birth, but
I wanted to explore Rattler's Blight. I cut the corner
too fine, got caught between swells and struck bottom.

Instant panic. I don't know what is worse, the
sound of fiberglass on rock or the thought of being
snapped in two. Only forty five minutes before, I had
left with Ray's warnings of shoal ringing in my ears.
"Submerged rocks are easy to spot on windy days,
but may not even show a ripple during calm ones". It
was hopeless. The swell had deposited me between
two rocks and all I could do was hope and pray the
next one would free me. The water drained, gurgled
then roared back with a vengeance. Up and over. A
knee-jerk reaction had me pushing off the rocks with
the blade of my paddle. I was clear. It had been a
close call, my first with shoal water, but it wouldn't be
my last by a long shot.

At the head of Rattler's Blight, I stopped to visit
with the Allen family and yet more tea. The morning
had been full of wonderful generosity, simple and
unassertive, and before leaving my name had been
passed on by C.B. up the coast. I would be expected.

The next hurdle was Run by Guess. From sea
level the broken coastline of islands bordering

Pottle's Bay looked intimidating and the strange tidal currents, caused by their narrow passages, soon had me second guessing their directions. The day was still fine and the outlines of islands were clear and blue. Everything would have been perfect had it not been for some black ice floating just below the surface. I don't know where it came from, but it gave me the shock of my life. Two strikes in one day is two too many. It was last year's ice, probably from Lake Melville. It should have left weeks ago, but strong east winds must have delayed its departure.

I negotiated the passage through Run by Guess with no further problem then ran into a log jam of ice flows in Pottle's Bay. They came in all shapes and sizes and ranged in colour from snowy white to sky blue, from green to murky grey. Some had surfaces as sharp as kitchen knives and others, half melted, dark and sinister with rippled surfaces, lay almost submerged like mini-icebergs ready to be struck.

For those sailing north from the Strait of Belle Isle, the all-important question is, 'When will the ice be gone?' The harbours and inlets south of Hamilton are usually navigable by mid-June, and July north of it. This year it was late. Below average temperatures coupled with below average snow falls meant a late breakup. To compound the situation, on-shore winds kept the ice around longer than usual. I learned in Rigolet that Makkovik was still waiting for the Northern Ranger's first visit and by all accounts the waters from Cape Harrison to Cape Strawberry was still chock-a-block full of ice.

By early evening I'd paddled down Abliuk Bight, portaged the short neck of land to Holton Harbour and made camp. If I thought I'd seen ice before, what I now saw made the ice in Pottle's Bay look miniature.

The Labrador current not only influences the climate, but also responsible for one of its natural wonders; the iceberg. Manhattan in ice, served up on a sea of blue. The comparison of icebergs and sky-

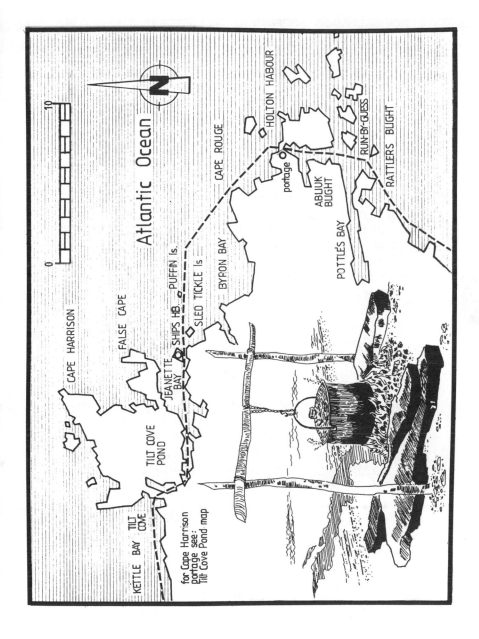

scrapers, is no idle observation. Their origins are from the ice fields around Greenland and Baffin Island and their gigantic sizes, eroded shapes and uncertain ages make them compelling viewing. The last thing I expected was to see them high and dry, but that's just what I saw. Like lemmings to the slaughter, the winds and tide had pushed them ashore. My snug little cove turned into a rush hour of ice. Even if I wanted to continue, there was no telling where the maze of small channels between the icebergs and the ice pans would take me.

I watched as huge ice flows, pushed in by the tide, buckled, cracked and reared out of the sea. Ice pans were rafting against one another in ridges, while others slowly turned belly-up, only to be nipped in the action of rolling over by their neighbour. The ocean had turned into a constantly changing landscape, a jagged mass of ice whose direction was in the hands of tidal currents and trade winds and whose noise from a distance sounded like a thousand chandeliers blowing in the wind.

I couldn't help it but the sea of ice triggered off my worst fear. Left with my thoughts, they inevitably returned to polar bears. The last thing I wanted was to turn in early. I'd camped in a shallow bed carpeted in moss. Low stunted ferns were few and far between, offering little if any shelter and a very poor harvest of fuel. I wanted to build a fire, a huge fire. I combed the beach from sunset to twilight and didn't let up the search until I had enough wood for a bonfire. It didn't last long. A fine mist rolled in from the sea, turned to rain and the last I remembered was watching my fire hiss and sparkle under the rain drops.

The wind and tide had changed during the night and so had the ice. With the exception of two grounded icebergs, the cove was free and what sea swell there was had been muffled by its off shore band of ice. Paddling is paradise when smooth waters turn to natural mirrors. The early morning mist had vapourised and now turned into a mirage. Island colours, lifted off their rocks, now hung above the ice in a washy haze of green and brown.

Today offered a catalogue of wild life: seals, hundreds of them; spotted harp and the larger-than-life square flipper. They dotted the off-shore ice like freckles, popping up here and there, all sad-eyed like those of a wet puppy dog. Maybe it was a case of safety in numbers or maybe they'd never been hunted before by a bright yellow kayak. They were fearless. Only the females, suntanning themselves, made any attempt to get away and as soon as the danger passed they were struggling to get back onto the ice.

At Cape Rouge, my trip almost came to an ignominious end. It was time for a break and I chose to beach on a small island behind a 'growler'. I chose the rock and ice over the shoreline to get away from the mosquitoes. The next I remembered was a grinding noise. My cat-nap was cut short. The wind and tide had changed again. My kayak, secured by rope from rocks, was entombed in small chunks of bergy ice and the growler, once at a safe distance, was now dangerously close. Ten more minutes and my kayak would have been so much crushed Easter Egg.

The day's second mistake found me setting off across Byron Bay on the wrong bearing. I mistook Ship's Head Island for the mainland - an honest mistake, considering the heat and haze. Two hours later I was ten miles out resting up on Puffin Island. I wasn't worried. I still felt fresh and with a tail wind and an impressive view of Cape Harrison, what else could I ask? Sixty minutes later my mistake turned into a glorious surprise. Puffins, thousands of them, with distinctive nut-cracking red beaks.They came in waves. I had paddled into a rainbow coloured bird sanctuary.

It was close to sunset before I made Ship's Head Harbour. I'd been on the sea for over twelve hours and felt none the worse for it. The day's heat had

massaged my back and my wrists, sore and swollen
from the battle down Lake Melville, had returned to
their normal size. Even my skin rash had healed and
its cause, my tight fitting wetsuit, now molded to my
skin like an old glove. I still suffered the occasional
leg cramp, but slowly my body and mind were
adjusting to their new home.

That night I watched Cape Harrison turn pink
under a spectacular sunset. It looked a fearsome
obstacle. Reaching out like an angry arm, it was
everything I had imagined. If I thought my earlier
conquest of open water was like tight-rope walking,
then the route round Cape Harrison was a free fall
into the unknown. I'm a raging romantic, mad, bad
and dangerous, but not stupid. Capes may sound
idyllic to the story teller in me, but are the kiss of
death to my kayaking psyche. Six months ago I had
made a pact with myself not to go around Cape
Harrison, no matter how calm the seas were. I can
put up with all kinds of physical pain, but mental
anguish in the form of nightmares is another story.
Lake Melville had proved my metal, but a promise is
a promise and the night I spent on Ship's Harbour
Island was used going over final details of my
portage route behind the Cape. I was going to follow
the winter ski-doo route down Jeanette Bay, take
Bob's Brook, cross Tilt Cove Pond, then drag, carry or
pull my kayak over three miles of open country to the
sea beyond. No easy task at the best of times, but
then I didn't know I was about to triple my burden.

Chapter 16
Bernie's Folly

I HAD ALL KINDS OF MAPS -TOPOGRAPHICAL, sea charts; some 1: 50,000 and others 1: 250,000. Every inch of coastline was covered, or so I thought. The brook that led to the pond at the back of Cape Harrison was at the bottom of a horseshoe cove at the end of Jeanette Bay. My maps showed both the north and south shores of the bay at its mouth, but the bottom of the bay tapered off and a small corner was missing. This portion continued on another map, a map I didn't have - and this was to prove my downfall

It took me just two hours to paddle down Jeanette Bay and ten minutes to find the brook. It was now 11:00 a.m. I had visions of completing the portage in one day, and I was too eager to get on with it. I should have double checked, but instead I immediately halved the load in my kayak, filled my waterproof back-pack and set off pulling my kayak up the brook.

The first seeds of doubt that I was on the wrong brook entered my mind when it shaved off into a stream. Then, one hour later, it turned into a dark liquid path overgrown with willows and fallen trees. By 5:00 p.m. only my stubborn pride kept me going forward. My map showed the brook winding over an area less than a mile long. I knew I was going slowly, but surely not that slowly. By 7:00 p.m. I was getting desperate. The brook had levelled off into a swamp and mosquitoes were driving me crazy. By now I was exhausted. One moment I would be knee deep in mud, the next high and dry carrying my kayak over rocks. I had to cut down willows, move fallen trees and sometimes wade waist deep in frigid pools of water. That night I camped on top of a large

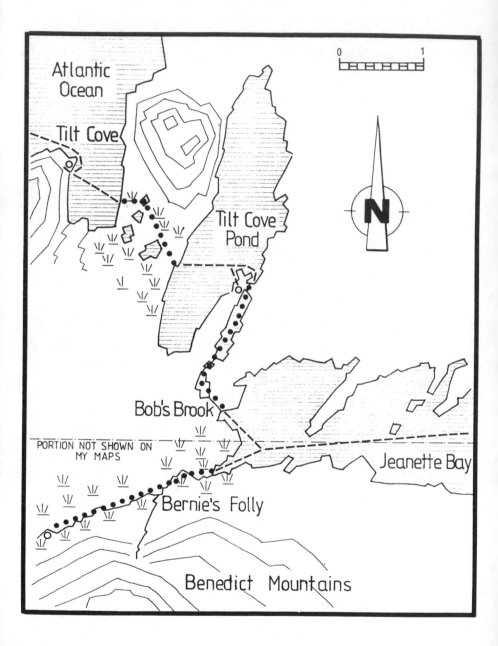

table-shaped rock in the swamp and by nightfall the inside of my tent looked like a blotting pad with red inky patches marking mosquito kills.

At first light, I took off up the side of a mountain only to have my worst fears confirmed. In the distance, due east of my present position, and clearly outlined against a border of trees, was Tilt Cove Pond. I could even trace Bob's Brook back down to Jeanette Bay. I was up the wrong brook. Bernie's folly!

There was nothing to do but go back. I wasn't depressed, just angry with myself for not checking my route earlier. It took me two and a half hours to cover the same distance I had so stubbornly covered in seven the day before. That was on the plus side. On the minus, I holed the kayak on the way down. Sea kayaks, I learned the hard way, are not designed to take rapids. I hit a submerged tree, ended up broadsiding a rock and spinning on another before hitting a third and capsizing. What an adventure, and it only got better.

Back in Jeanette Bay, I went over my map with a fine tooth comb. The brook I had taken was identical in size and shape. Obviously there were two, within a few hundred yards of each other. I was that close, but close isn't good enough.

By late afternoon I had made Tilt Cove Pond, done what epoxy repair work on the hole I could, and called it a day. It wasn't a complete success, it still leaked a bit, but nothing more than a sponge job. It would be an irritant, but at least the kayak wouldn't sink.

The next day I got lost again. Well, not quite. I was just looking for those tell tale signs on the other side of the pond that told me others had passed this way before on ski-doo.

It's only a fool, or the naive who hides his trail. In Toronto hidden behind street signs and food wrappings are the background hums of civilization. You take it all for granted when you live in it. It's easy to forget, but if you're lost, miles from nowhere, in the pristine wonder of mother nature, even a Mars bar wrapper, empty Coke tin or gas tank can be a life saver. I'm not trying to promote litter, but there's nothing more pleasing to the eye than seeing some-one else's cast offs, even if it be litter, after hours of searching for a trail. I've been straightened out by gas containers nailed to trees before now and, let's face it, a can of Pepsi is still the best sign of civilization known to man, so when I saw two empty tins of Vienna sausages, I knew I was on the right track. The next three hours were spent scouting out the portage route from pond to cove and marking the trail with surveyors' tape. I wasn't about to make the same mistake twice.

My portage followed caribou moss wherever pos-sible. I could use it to slide my kayak over, and before starting, I duct-taped over my kayak's epoxy repair work to protect it.

The kayak full loaded weighed over two hundred and fifty pounds, so I broke it down to three loads. With two black-sacks and an empty kayak, it meant every yard covered would in reality be six yards walked. It was a long day, but by early evening I was within spitting distance of the sea.

Ever since leaving the pond, I'd seen fresh bear droppings. I took to carrying my shotgun with every load. I hate saying it but it made me feel safe and equalized the playing field. Now, within yards of the beach, I got careless.

Ever been caught with your trousers down? Well, that's just how I felt when I saw this huge black bear without my shotgun. It looked as surprised as me, but was a whole lot bigger and in the bush the old saying 'the biggest rules' means just that.

I could hardly walk, let alone run. I shouted, it grunted. It wasn't intimidated in the slightest. They never seem to act like in the text books when you want them to. I dropped my load, walked, then tried to run. I was exhausted and by the time I reached my shotgun cardiac arrest set in. I hardly had the energy to lift, let alone point, aim and fire my shotgun, and by the time I got my breath, settled my nerves and retraced my steps back to the beach, it was gone. I'm not an animal lover at the best of times and when a red fox popped its head up I'd had enough excitement for one day.

I made camp on the northside of Tilt Cove. The sight of a derelict house beckoned and no sooner was the tent up, than I set off down the beach to explore.

In a land where wilderness reigns supreme, human habitation when left unattended returns to nature in double quick time. Wood and shrub can swallow life signs in a few generations and any site, · no matter how small, begs investigation. The long house viewed from a distance turned into three derelict homes and the distant pile of grey, wind-burned wood into a beached and broken boat. I trod on an old buck saw, stumbled over a pile of rusty cans, then unearthed a double-bladed axe. One door was still on its hinges, but he roofs had long since collapsed and the elements had worn down the rest. In a few more generations all evidence that people lived here will be rubbed out. The wood will end up entombed in moss and the nails will sink into the earth. It will go from historical site to geological discovery in our grandchildren's lifetime, but one object will remain on the surface like a tombstone. Every spring its roots will burst into life, its leaves will force their way to the surface and its shooting stem will will thicken and then ripen ready for picking. The Labrador rhubarb garden is indestructible.

I was just about to leave when I struck gold. I found some screwed-up pages of newspaper in a wall void. 'War is declared', Hindenberg Disaster' or maybe 'Newfoundland joins Canada'. Dollar signs flashed through my head. This piece of paper could be my ticket home. I could just see myself, front row at Sotheby's. 'Any more bids $10,000 once, $10,000 twice.'..!, then I saw the date, Jan 10th 1991! It was a recent copy of the Labradorian, not even worth the paper it was printed on.

Chapter 17
A Rising Land

THANKGOD FOR SMALL MERCIES.THE FIRST hint of ice came with the morning fog. There wasn't a breath of air and you couldn't buy a breeze for love or money. The sun had risen hours ago. I was half way across Kettle Bay, yet the sea was still asleep. I was paddling in an eerie graveyard of ice. The sun had shattered into a thousand fragments and all forms appeared dark and frosty. Picking lanes through the ice floes was hopeless. Cape Strawberry was still hidden in haze and keeping a set course was impossible. Once again I was forced to zig-zag. The ice extended in all directions plus thousands of growlers, ice pans and the floating garbage of bergy bits. Some ice floes had silver pinnacles and purple caves and some, with green iridescent ice beaches, roared back every time a swell rubbed against them. Some were of the sit-up and beg variety, small with smooth sculptured surfaces, and some cathedral like gothic and austere. Some were energetic, ready to split, and bobbed and waved in the slightest current, while others, huge in stature, floated by like prehistoric monsters. Twice the ice hid the sight and sounds of passing speed boats. Like radio waves, noise fades in and out behind solid objects. One moment an engine roared, the next baffled out, obscured behind ice. It was frustrating. Four days without human contact.

On one occasion, I was caught exploring an iceberg. The speed boat went one side, I the other and its resultant wake had me paddling like crazy. When an iceberg does make a noise, it's a thunder clap. It started with a crack. At first I thought the speed boat's owner was out on a seal hunt, but the next sound literally burst my ear drums. The noise jerked

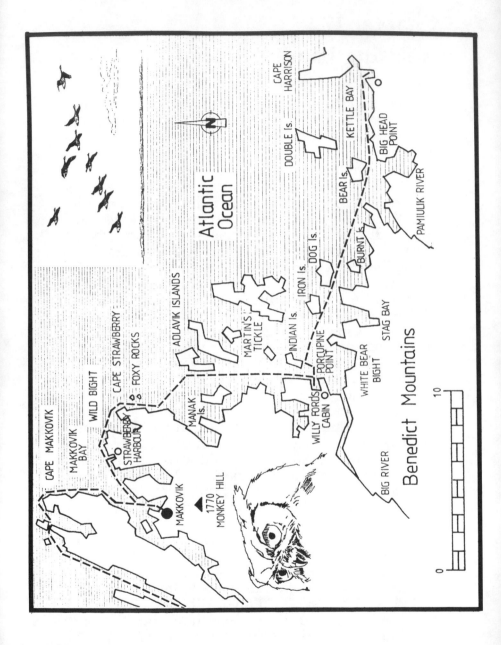

my head around just in time to see a slab of ice drop
vertically, half sink then roll onto its side. No sooner
had my eyes focused than another explosion hit the
iceberg. For almost a minute the iceberg rocked slowly back and forth. Then came the wave. It crept up, a
a white line of slow motion power. Seconds later, I
was lifted. A graceful curved picked up the kayak
like a feather, rocked it, flattened, then continued its
chain reaction, influencing everything in its wake.

By Big Head Point the ice floes had thinned out
and past Bear Island the only objects that weren't
topped with green were a few grounded ice icebergs
and the occasional growler. It was high noon. The
sun just hovered, all heat and glare. It turned Adlavik
Islands into a heat haze of jellied blobs and fried my
mind inside out. I was boiling: the sun bored into my
back and my wet suit turned into a prison of sweat.

Who sits naked on a rock, singing to a beach of
empty seats? I do. If anyone passed, they would have
found me a candidate for the nut house. I couldn't
help it. I was steaming. The heat undressed me. Even
the cold sea water, not much above 40 deg F. offered
only relief.

From hot sauna to cold shower; instant rejuvena-
tion. Then the itching started. Since Rigolet, I'd
unknowingly acquired a few unwanted passengers.
My cold water swim had woken them up, now they
were complaining. I'm not a clean freak. I believe in
letting the layers of sweat and dirt build up, but as I
found the hard way, it may be great protection
against mosquitoes, but a veritable breeding ground
for fleas. For thirty minutes I soaped, swam and
sponged my way to cleanliness and by the time I'd
finished, my passengers had been sent to a watery
grave.

By sunset the wavy mirages had straightened out,
lines had returned to normal and the Labrador sea to
its turquoise blue. I was now spoiled for choice.
There were fish cabins to all points of the compass:
Indian Island, Big River and Porcupine Point. I was

drifting in open water across Stag Bay, waiting to hear the tell-tale signs of life. I didn't have to wait long. A speed boat sent me in the direction of Indian Island, but no sooner had I reached its source than the noise did a U turn and headed off towards Porcupine Point. Immediately I turned into its sound, followed it into silence, then waited. Once again it set off in a different direction, this time Big River. It was like being caught in the Bermuda Triangle. I was disappearing down my own indecision. I was too lazy to make camp on my own and too proud to keep the experience of the Cape Harrison portage to myself. I was bursting with stories and wanted someone to share them with. The scene was now like a John Wayne movie with the exception of his horse. I was paddling into the sunset. The sky was blood red and the block of land in front deep purple. The water was perfectly calm and the reflections in it jet black. The Benedict Mountain range had turned into a jagged silhouette and as the sun exited, pale blues turned royal and violet hues streaked the sky. I was kayaking in a picture of extremes; even the noise of my paddle cutting through the water was razor sharp. I'd been paddling for ten hours. My body was spent, but my brain gave out different signals. Then the full moon rose. Instantly, colours bleached. It sounds corny now, but had I not been spotted, I would have gladly spent the night at sea anchored to kelp. I was so absorbed in the experience that anything felt possible. I was beginning to relax into my kayak and it seemed to be returning the compliment. It was just one of those 'LARGE LABRADOR DAYS' when everything goes right.

I spent the night camped by the side of Willy Ford's cabin. His family provided the audience and, while they wined and dined me, I entertained them with every tall story in my repertoire.

That evening I couldn't escape the moon. It illuminated the tent like a fluorescent light bulb, followed my head and pricked my eyes at every turn.

Its disc influenced everything - the animals, the tide and now myself.

So far, I had only been caught out once by the tide. Even though the tide varies little over four feet, I got caught high and dry at Lowlands Point and ended up having to drag my fully loaded kayak over a combination of sand, mud and rock. Until now I had been spoiled for choice. I could always find a sandy beach, but by the look of the layered steps of rock down Cape Strawberry, from now on sheltered beaches would be few and far between.

I woke to a turbulent sky. Flashes of white on rough sea underscored the drama above. The coast-line was forever changing, so now was the weather, and with it so was my mood. Should I, or shouldn't I? Yesterday, Cape Strawberry looked calm, colourful and inviting, today it looked like an angry arm of solid rock. I'd come a long way since Holton Harbour but it wasn't until Cape Harrison that I sensed a change in landscape. I had passed the same jagged shore before, the same ground cover, the same absence of trees, but now the land was beginning to rise. The softly curved hills now gave way to naked cliffs and the rises of snow-patched land in the distance could almost be called mountains.

At the last minute I decided to risk the weather and take the inside passage up Long Island Tickle. All morning I paced myself. I was holding something in reserve just in case the weather turned ugly and I needed to put on a spurt. I didn't want to hang about rounding the cape, and Wild Bight's name didn't exactly fill me with confidence. Manak Island marked the end of the rope; from this point there was no turning back.From here the Cape dropped in smooth tiers straight into the sea. I would have nothing to hold onto and Fox Islands weren't safe havens of harbour. At least the elements were in my favour. The wind had died and with no back swells to worry about, I could hug the shoal with no problem. I now had one eye trained on the clouds and one on the rocks ahead. Everything was fine. The sun came and went like a Peeping Tom and the off shore winds were moderate. The first signs of trouble ahead came when a dull sheen glazed the sky. The atmosphere thickened and I saw the first evidence of choppy waters below Lookout Point. I snuck back in for one last rest. My timing couldn't have been worse, for as I rested the clouds darkened.

To say I could have made Makkovik that night would be stretching it. True, the wind and tide were in my favour, but that was now and no-one could predict what the weather had in store when the sun set. Those invisible borders of influence called coastal currents are a law unto themselves and sudden squalls can throw a spanner in any well-meaning equation. When the sun drops, up and down drafts can turn water corridors like Makkovik Bay from glass calm to raging wind tunnels within minutes. It all starts when cold air rubs up against a hot surface and that time was closing in rapidly. I was surrounded by huge rocks of radiant heat and the sun had already dropped behind their shadow. It's enough to brave the elements without bravado creeping into my life and, as if to push my decision over the edge, no sooner had I poked my nose out of Nipper Cove a sudden blast of air almost capsized me. I immediately down scaled my planned arrival that day in Makkovik and felt myself lucky to find shelter when I did. The wind soon accelerated to a full-scale squall and Strawberry Harbour couldn't come quickly enough. I put up my tent in double quick time and then set about quelling my humongous appetite.

For me there are no half measures. Feast or famine, that's my motto. After all, I would be able to replenish my stores in Makkovik, so I started off with beans and rice, then polished off my remaining tub of 'stick to your ribs' unique recipe of peanut butter, honey and full-fat powdered milk. Stupid mistake. All night my stomach talked. Needless to say, many things happened that night and by sunrise the evidence of my over indulgence decorated the campsite.

It goes without saying that my days were lonely except for the settlements. Human sightings were rare. Ships, fishing boats and people were few and far between. Communities may be only hours apart by speed boat, but are days apart by paddle power. I had spent seven days at sea since leaving Rigolet. At night the coastal AM/FM radio stations emitted a steady stream of static and only the Canadian Broadcasting Corporation's short wave was clear. Generally I had the feeling of being entirely on my own. However, this is not the reality. On the rare occasions I was spotted, or went ashore,I realized that although I may not have been aware of anyone else on the coast, lots of people were aware of me, and what I was up to. So it was when I crossed paths with Coon Anderson and his pal coming up Ford's Bight en route home to Makkovik. He'd been forewarned of my coming, but obviously, from the looks I was about to receive, ignorant of my vices.

"Have you a light, mate?" I've been mistaken for a keep-fit maniac, vegetarian, social worker, federal spy and an explorer with a death wish, but my vices have never been questioned.

I could have knocked them over with a feather. Where else does the unspoken word speak volumes. Once again I had arrived with the sweat of travel on my clothes and once again it became the key to people's hearts and homes. No sooner had I beached in Makkovik than I found myself surrounded by cheerful kitchen chatter and the mouthwatering smells of Fiona Anderson's cooking.

Only 160 miles separate Makkovik by boat from Rigolet, yet one only had to glance at the telephone directory and count the Andersons of Norwegian descent listed in its pages to see the difference. I had entered a community founded on traditional values, fiercely proud and in no small part buttressed against change by the dangerous waters of Cape Harrison. It was love at first sight. Maybe it was its secure harbour, sheltered by two outpoints like welcoming arms. Maybe it was its neat cluster of houses topped by blue smoke or maybe it was the carpet of green set below an imposing range of bald hills. I think not. My love affair started and ended in the kitchen. With these people there was no excuse for haste and who was I to break with tradition? One day slipped into two and I was into the third day before I got my act together.

I holed my kayak again in Strawberry Harbour. Two folds of rock united below a swell. Now it required additional repairs. I also had letters to write, mail to pick up and provisions to purchase, but most of all I wanted to stretch, unwind and celebrate. If the truth be told, I never really expected to get further than Rigolet. I thought my nerves would give out at the first blue horizon. Now, the thought of paddling all the way up the Labrador coast was a definite reality.

As a piece of coastal trivia, outside of Mary's Harbour and Cartwright, 'Susie's Boarding House', in the name of Susie Anderson, held the only 'off premises' drinking license on the coast. It was a bridge, I was told, not easily crossed. Everyone knows that it's foolish to give alcohol to men with time to fill and even worse to people like myself who are not use to it, but one cannot relax, celebrate and be sensible all at the same time. Luckily for me, I caught Susie in a receptive mood. She'd heard of my exploits on the radio. I was a hit and could do no wrong and left thirty minutes later with a six pack, dutifully concealed in a plastic bag.

Celebrations over, I got down to the serious business of kayak repair. First I had to strip off the temporary seal of duct tape, then sand down the earlier epoxy repair job from the Cape Harrison portage. That was the easy part. I remembered some guide book advice to wilderness kayakers: 'Equipment should be simple and basically sound. If it fails, you will probably be the one to repair it.' My equipment fit the bill but my repair kit fell short.

"None left, boy." I'd entered the government store with high hopes, but the word, 'none', hit my panic button. "We got more coming on the next boat."

"Next boat! When's that?"

"It depends on the ice, boy." I now remembered the next gem of guide book information. 'Supplies of all kinds are still pretty limited in both variety and quantity by city standards. Almost everything has to be either shipped or flown in under special order at great expense.' What a time to remember! The store had two industrial-sized cans of fiberglass resin, enough cloth to coat a speed boat, but no hardening agent. I left empty handed, but not without hope. Word went out that the 'tourist' was in trouble. 'You know, the 'WALKING MAN' from winter,' and before the morning was out, help arrived and by supper my kayak was as good as new.

The next port of call was to the Fish and Wild Life Office. Whatever else a man on the coast is or does you can count on it that he's also tied to the fishing season. Fishing is still the principal occupation during the short summer. Fish and weather constitute seven tenths of the subject matter discussed and I had learned more about the local tides, safe harbours, currents, winds and rocks than any amount of printed material could give me.Erick Anderson was no exception. We spent the best part of an afternoon going over suitable routes and by evening I was packed and ready to leave on the morning tide.

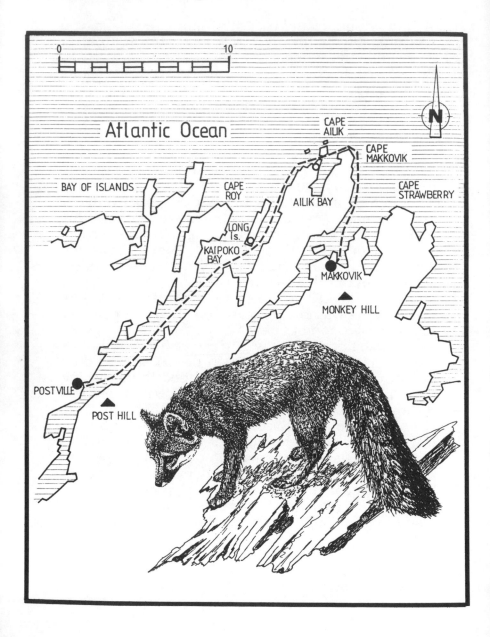

0   10

Atlantic Ocean

CAPE
AILIK

CAPE
MAKKOVIK

N

BAY OF ISLANDS

CAPE
ROY

AILIK BAY

CAPE
STRAWBERRY

LONG
Is.

KAIPOKO
BAY

MAKKOVIK

MONKEY HILL

POSTVILLE

POST HILL

Chapter 18
Visions of Greenland

IF I'D STAYED ANOTHER DAY NO ONE WOULD have been offended. The sky looked dark and angry and Makkovik Bay didn't look much better. The wind came out of the north west, played havoc with the tidal swells and streaked the bay like a zebra's back. Just before Measle's Point a sudden squall hit. I didn't have the time to react, let alone be frightened. It happened so quickly and with such force that it stole my hat, blew the map case into my face and tore the paddle out of my hands. It caught me at the top of a swell, swung me round like a compass needle and left me 45 degrees off course. The writing was on the wall, but it look infinitely safer to go forward rather than turning back.

The Bay looked a mess in comparison to the Cape. I was now betting the winds would stay offshore and that Cape Makkovik would act as a wind break. For once, I was right. The wind eventually blew itself out, the clouds dispersed and by noon the gulls were playing in a fiery sun. I was now paddling in a picture postcard of smooth rock and imposing cliffs. My confidence was soaring. One Cape doesn't a kayaker make, but in less than one week I'd pushed the borders of my experience further than I ever dreamed possible.

There's nothing worse than over-confidence. I'd been patting myself on the back all the way up Cape Makkovik. I had escaped a soaking, guessed right about the wind and now took the shelter for granted. I thought the worst was over. I even planned to by-pass the exposed lip of Cape Ailik, take the sheltered route down its Bay, then cut through Summer Cove. I should have weighed up the situation at the mouth of the Bay before attempting to cross. The warning signs were all there; a 'V' shaped pass between high hills, black clouds and a north westerly wind gearing up for a return visit. I expected foul weather, but it looked some time off. However, for it to strike so suddenly, with such prolonged force and at the bottom of the day when my tanks were dry, was just too much. It caught me in the middle of the bay. Was it a sick joke? Was I being punished for my over-confidence? I was by all accounts in easy waters. Ailik Bay isn't even a mile wide. What if I was caught out crossing Bay of Islands, Windy Tickle or paddling down the unpredictable Hopedale Run? If this region was soft and easy in comparison, perhaps I should listen to the voices of caution screaming in my head and call it quits in Postville. The abstract question didn't last long. I was quickly running out of land. I was being blown diagonally off course and now had visions of Greenland, Iceland and an unscheduled crossing of the Atlantic. The wind was funnelling down like a blast tunnel. It shaved the heads off swells, chopped up the surface and filled the air with spit. I was digging in like crazy and angling for balance. My wrists were burning and my back and shoulders didn't bear thinking about. My pace was erratic and the sight of land slowly slipping away only made matters worse. I was making it up as I went along. The text books say, 'go with the wind, put out a dragger anchor, and let the wind run its course'. If I did that, I could end up miles from shore in the sea lanes. I was lucky. A window of calm, a final sprint and a toe hold on land. I took some breathing space. Time to get a second wind and choose my poison. It looked risky, but not impossible, to beach. Catching the right swell was easy, the problem would be getting out of the kayak and pulling it to safety on bare rock, before the wrong one came along. I was in a no-man's land where the Cape tapered into the sea. I was in deep water and if I stayed centered I would be fine. Then a swell crested. It frightened me to death. I was lifted, pushed forward, then sucked out into the open. There was only one way to go , forward. I was now paddling head on into the wind and every time a swell picked me up another was ready and waiting to soak me. I made Summer Cove at a snail's pace. I was battered and bruised, but what an adventure. Sixty minutes later, I was asleep.

While my contemporaries in elementary school were escaping into the comic strip pages of Batman and Robin, I was into Moby Dick. It was a great fantasy to fall into as a child, but not as an adult.
WHOOSH......................A black shiny mass curved effortlessly out of the water not two hundred yards away before disappearing in a silent wake. My first whale sighting. It's one thing to be in awe at the safe side of a television screen and another to be floating around in the same pond. A sixty pound kayak is no match for two tons of blubber and no amount of Greenpeace propaganda could change the fact. The first snippet of useless information to enter my head was that whales have in-built radar systems. But I wasn't about to test this whale's ability or its goodwill. We were both hugging the shore on a collision course. It was no contest. My arms turned into windmills and had it not been for my rudder system, I would have turned into just another accident statistic. Thank God it didn't make any difference which way I turned. I slammed my foot down hard, nearly took the pedal off its hinges and shot straight in front of the diving whale.
True to my character, it didn't take long for cockiness to return. I was already writing the next chapter when another popped into view, then another. I know most people would give their eye teeth to experience a whale, but when you're on your own, safety is uppermost. I sprinted ashore, lit a fire and had a brew-up. I was spell-bound. Not three ,but five whales passed. For thirty minutes they circled the waters off Brent's Cove, then disappeared. The incident left me a little weak. Who knows where they

went, or if they would be return?

The day was cut short by fog. An early morning rainshower had steamed, road the updrafts; clouded the hills, then burst. It was now falling with the barometer. It started like a whispering ghost, picked up momentum down Kaipoko Bay and now hid all except the lines between land and sea. It was a splendid isolation. A hush descended, weird shapes floated in and out of vision and a penetrating dampness only added to the ocean scents. Had the fog rolled in anywhere else, I would have been worried. It didn't last long. A fine drizzle turned to rain, to drops as big as your knuckle. It turned the glass calm into a cauldron of bubbles. I beached, made camp on Long Island in double quick time, then lay back into its relentless patter.

Postville had been a last minute addition to my itinerary. Located over thirty miles down from Kaipoko Bay, I chose it for its deep fiord-like inlet, its sheltered corridor and its arctic char. In Toronto, Postville was just a spot on a map, a question mark among many and, outside of Marine Atlantic summer schedules, non-existent until recently. Hard to believe now, but in the autumn of '92 a poster advertising 'COME TO LABRADOR BEFORE THE TOURISTS.' would have hit the spot. That's not to say there wasn't any information on Labrador. The Torngat Mountain range is no secret and Labrador's big game hunting and fishing is known from Tokyo to Texas. Students of history have read their Doctor Grenvilles and the Moravian missionaries and the 'Lure of the Wild' is still standard reading in most North American libraries. But sadly, the Postvilles of this world don't get the recognition they deserve. They have no historical sites to sell, no gold in their river and Big Foot hasn't been seen since the last batch of homebrew. Postville is just an ordinary place full of extraordinary people and it wasn't until I got to Goose Bay and unearthed a government subsi-

dized book on coastal statistics that I found the information I was looking for.

POSTVILLE

.... named it Postville because it had been
the location of the Hudson Bay company trading post
and had always been referred to as 'The Post'.
Location: 113 air miles from Goose Bay.
Population: 190
Infrastructure: Power, Nfld/Labrador hydro
Water: Wells, community dam
Sewage: Septic tanks and honey bucket
Soil structure: Sand, gravel and bedrock
Fuel: Stove oil and gasoline/local agent
Transportation
Air: Labrador Airways
Marine: CN coastal boats
Local: Snowmobiles, boats and trucks
Communication
Telephone: Nfld telephone (operator handled)
Radio/TV: C.B.C. radio, C.B.C. TV.
Mail: Local post office, A0P 1N0
Facilities/Services.
Medical: Nursing station, one nurse
Religion: Pentecostal and Moravian
Education: Pentecostal school, five teachers K - 11
Housing: Private and Federal/Provincial funded
Retail outlets: 1 general store, 1 variety
Public accommodation: Local hospitality
Recreation: Ball field, outdoor rink, playground
Resource industry: Fishery, shipyard and sawmill
Summer stations: Ailik, Barr Harbour, Black Is.

Little has changed since the information was published in the early '60s. Hospitality and the fisheries
are still its mainstay and its picturesque Inlet its
biggest draw. True phones are in almost every home
and direct dialing is the norm. C.B.C. television
comes in loud and clear and cable T.V. is just around
the corner. Having said that, Postville, like many

other coastal communities, is an afterthought in most people's itinerary.

It took me one and a half days to cover the distance from Ailik to Postville down Kaipoko Bay. From the Sisters' Island the inlet narrowed sharply and its sides responded by rising. Here and there, I could see evidence of forest fires. Fires in Labrador are fairly common. Lodge Bay, Charlottetown and the one in Goose Bay came perilously close to the community. They happen quickly, sometimes when least expected, but due to the lack of coastal density, are rarely long or extensive. Usually they do no more than singe off spruce needles, but once scarred these trees suffocate quickly and die. From a distance a wind burn looks like a regiment of stick skeletons. Grey in colour and stripped of bark, dead spruce makes ideal kindling wood, burning quick and hot and is much sought after. I even heard of people coming from as far afield as Hopedale, a distance of 100 miles by boat. A long way by anyone's standards.

I was now kayaking in Post Hill's shadow. Cubes of colour were clearly visible, then came the speed boats, the smell of smoke and the noise of children. I arrived to a busy wharf. Wide-eyed and curious and exuding youthful energy, the children fell over themselves to help. Then a 4-wheeler came and all eyes turned to the man harnessed behind its wheel. It was Herb Manak arriving to welcome another visitor.

To understand the story behind Herb's specially converted 4-wheeler is to gain a unique insight into the close-knit communities of Labrador's north shore. In an age of multi-media telethons, bandaid concerts and faceless causes, it came as a breath of fresh air to know that community self-help is alive and well. Labrador's history is steeped in self-sacrifice, of shared grief and shared joy, but if I thought its spirit had been dispatched to the pages of folk lore, Herb and his 4-wheeler proved me wrong.

Herb recently lost both his legs to bad blood circulation. He was an outdoorsman but it now looked like he would become a prisoner to immobility. Then the community in Postville started fund-raising. Pot - luck suppers, bake and craft sales and door to door collections raised the money and three thousand two hundred dollars later the community gave Herb back his independence.

"Hop on boy, I'll take you to see the Rev." Two minutes later Herb dropped me at the Reverend's door and by the end of the day I'd passed from Reverend to teacher to layman and by supper time I'd become the adopted son of the Jaques' household.

News travels in many ways up and down the coast but when Doris Jaques shot up from the supper table to answer a crackling noise, another unique piece of coastal jigsaw slotted into place. The 'trail radio' system has been in northern Labrador since 1985. The radio, Doris told me, was mostly used by people who go inland to hunt or trap commercially, or by fisherman who go to their summer camps up and down the coast for long periods of time. The high frequency radio provides the hunters and fisher-men with basic communications in case of emer-gency, or lets their relatives know that they have arrived safely at their destination. For six months I had experienced one side of the coin. From Mikey Pottle to Willy Ford the fish cabin C.B. had been my life line of communication. I was passed down its wave lengths; 'The walking man's coming'; 'Keep an eye out for a yellow boat.' Now, in the Jaques' house, I was to experience its base station.

The base allows the users to talk from radio to telephone - not always clear, as Doris said, but better than nothing. Ranges of 100 to 200 miles are not uncommon, but some days it can be crystal clear and on others the noise level so bad you can't hear your-self think. Today was average and so was its news. 'How's the baby?' 'Not many salmon, boy', and the inevitable 'As the kayakman arrived?' I was begin-ning to wish I had invested in a portable radio; life insurance, cheap at half the price.

Day two started with a lazy morning fish. I am no rod and reel expert. I could never understand catch and release or the so-called sportsmen who get their jollies by playing fish for all they're worth. I even have some friends who swear to the sport's soothing qualities and its Zen-like insights.

Fishing is not one of my primary pastimes, but when the fish are biting and you catch two good-size arctic char and three trout in less than thirty minutes, I will take it. Next it was rock cod jigging and then a trip to some gill nets and fresh salmon. I didn't think life could get better but then Tolsten Jaques offered me his family cabin on Kaipoko River. For the next three days I closed the door on travel. I could eat and sleep when I wanted and hear only the sounds of my own thoughts. The days passed all too quickly and before I knew it I was back in the cockpit paddling east up Kaipoko Bay en route to my next stop, Hopedale.

Chapter 19
Weather waits for No-One

IF I TAKE MY CUE FROM THE SURROUNDINGS then the day went like a dream. The sky was cloudless; light blue, with just enough breeze to make paddling comfortable. My plan was to cut out Cape Roy and take advantage of the winter ski-doo trail from Bay of Islands to Kaipoko Bay. It worked like a charm.

Iggiuk Bight opened like a page in a book. Two faces, one coated in lush green and the other in naked rock. For two miles it both tapered in and jutted out of the water before shaving off in a neck of low land. Once again I had exchanged open waters for shelter, and a short dry portage for an exposed point. Once again I was rewarded. Last night's frost had grounded the mosquitoes and black fly were non-existent. The half mile portage through a treeless corridor was a piece of cake and its six miles of interconnecting salt water ponds turned into a rich musical landscape of wild life

Most people - and I am no different - base their impressions of wilderness through the lens of TV documentaries. Action is the name of the game and movement is all important. The idea is to grip the viewer in the very first scene and keep his attention by a sequence of overlapping experiences. These programs are far from the truth. Until today my trip had been one long interlude of slow motion travel punctuated by the occasional distraction. Human contact was rare and wildlife sightings few and far between. But there were exceptions to the rule and today proved to be one of them. Loons were everywhere. I must have spotted half a dozen pairs of harlequins, two colonies of nesting eider ducks, as well as king fishers and one huge bird of prey that watched me

Atlantic Ocean

HOPEDALE
ANNIOWAKTOOK Is.
HOPEDALE RUN

KINGITOK ISLANDS

DEEP INLET

FLAGSTAFF TICKLE

CROSS Is.

WINSOR HARBOUR

KANAIRIKTOK BAY

BAY OF ISLANDS

CAPE ROY

portage

IGGIUK BIGHT

SISTER'S Is

POSTVILLE

POST HILL

0   10

from the top of a tree as I glided past. I startled a fox,
caught sight of a porcupine, then surprised two caribou. They didn't even give me a second glance and
took off as if on springs. They bounded effortlessly
through shallow water, trotted through a bog as if it
didn't exist, before turning the speed up a notch on
dry land and disappearing into a thick thatch of bush.
The whole scene was a tapestry of rock, tundra and
tongues of wooded greenery that seemed to burst
into life on cue. I didn't know then, but the waterway
was under the tidal influence of a reversing rapid that
made its waters out of bounds for all but the adventurous. I was completely on my own and, being surrounded by high hills, totally cut off from man-made
noises. By late afternoon, I was camped just above
the rapids. Cape Roy's hills now dominated the view.
It was back to the coastal windswept look of bare rock
and twisted pines. I climbed the highest peak,
watched my watery corridor turn into an amber view,
but by midnight, I was struggling with sleep in a full
blown storm.

Dear Mum,
   Having a marvellous time....... There is one thing
worse than being caught out in a storm and that is
being stormbound with time on your hands and
nothing to fill it with. Now, if I was travelling with a
woman, there'd be no problem, but on your own it
can be as boring as hell. Everything irritates you.
Those loons that only last night called out in romantic tones now chatter incessantly and play on my
nerves. You cannot find that lone mosquito in your
tent and just when you get warm and dry you have to
go outside and take a leak! It all adds up to frustration. Your thoughts turn to all those little things that
now get completely blown out of proportion.
   My radio is dead and I can't find the spare batteries. That super sophisticated stove I bought in
Toronto that can burn everything from white gas to
rocket fuel is empty, and my tobacco, my one and

only vice on this trip, is running out.

I did make a lame attempt to search for dry wood, but this was cut short when, to my horror, the tent flew. Lighting a fire is one thing, having one's tent air-lifted to Greenland like a balloon is quite another. Even the tide was laughing at me, for no sooner had I secured the tent than I noticed my kayak drifting out to sea. At times like this, you want to cry. Nothing seems to go right. Sleep holds no escape, and even those chocolate biscuits I had been saving for over a month for just such an occasion had as much snap in them as a wet sponge.

Noon brought with it a window of light and a sudden surge in temperature. The flowers bloomed, waters calmed and the air was full of scent. But to venture out meant to run the gauntlet of black flies. They got everywhere. They got in your ears, up your nose and down your throat and just to make matters worse, I'd left the tent open and when I returned, I was bushwhacked by a swarm of mosquitoes.

It is said that you can hit a black fly with a base-ball bat and it will come back for more. They don't so much bite as mug you. Well let me tell you something. I have travelled all over Canada. I've worked in Grande Prairie, Alberta, Whitehorse, Yukon, Inuvik, NWT, Flin Flon, Manitoba, and Timmins in Ontario. I've been bitten, stung, battered and bruised by every species of winged creature known to man. But nothing comes close to the Labrador mosquito in an eating frenzy between storms. Here, they are that big they arm wrestle with you and the noise they make at night would make the 'Chainsaw Massacre' sound like a kiddies' nursery rhyme. That window of light proved to be the last straw. No sooner had I taken down the tent, than the weather closed in, the sky blackened, the winds blew and the rain sheeted down. White caps jumped out in the dull light and Bay of Islands looked suicidal. Once again, I had to put up the tent. There was nothing to do but grin and bear it. Then I found my spare batteries; at least I had my music.

It's best to think of the worst and count your blessings after. I act on the assumption that the weather waits for no-one. It's like catching a train. If you rush and get there with hours to spare, you can enjoy the wait and if you get there with only minutes to spare, you can enjoy the chase. The Bay of Islands was the biggest stretch of open water to date and as the morning was clear, I wasn't about to hang around watching to see if it would change.

I had been playing the dial since waking up. I missed the 6:00 a.m. fisheries broadcast to sleep and the 6:30 a.m. news to static. Today I would be taking a 15 mile diagonal course across open water and the weather forecast was an integral part of the day's decision. I was between stations. Yesterday afternoon, Makkovik's 103.5 FM came in loud and clear and in the evening it was Postville on 105.1 FM, but just when it mattered most, the airwaves went dead. It wasn't the first time wave bands overlapped or disappeared. In winter, I often got ball by ball commentary from Dodger Stadium when the Northern Lights were playing. It's the top of the ninth and 80 deg. F; strike two - smell the fresh grass. I could just picture myself; shades, bermuda shorts and a cool beer. This morning it was Hopedale's booster station on 91.1 FM. I had erected a makeshift aerial of snare wire. I was hedging my bets and when the weather forecast came through, I was off to the races.

I was now used to psychoanalyzing myself by a forecaster's report. Rained in - depression; strong north easterlies - grounded; sunny and clear-life couldn't be better. Today it was a touch of sunny with cloudy periods - no problemo.

The Bay of Islands is a sea with shores so far apart they are scarcely visible on hazy days. It greeted me with a dark silhouette. The three islands I was heading for, and Winsor Harbour in particular, were just visible through binoculars. I took a compass bearing, filed the horizon away, then almost immediately lost it to sun. By midday, shadows melted. Background and foreground fused. The group of three sank back into a dark band of mainland peaks and didn't give up their secrets until I was two thirds across. By then it was too late. The day's load had increased by three miles. I was heading for the wrong island.

To keep body and mind together during the long crossing, I took to ice flow hopping. It was my only yardstick for judging speed and once past, I would immediately lock on to another. It helped to keep my mind focused, gave me something to work towards and also encouraged me to sprint. Excess energy was a rarity at any time. I had spent 24 days in the cockpit. My biceps had hardened and my shoulders were a mass of protruding veins. But I still had little pain threshold in my upper body. Only once did I put on a sprint. I kept it going for ten minutes in calm conditions and at the end it felt like someone had jabbed a hot poker down my throat. I was a body in constant motion and even though it often ached, my senses were rarely dulled. I was alert to everything, the wind, the clouds. I even put down my deep sleeps more to the daily mental stress of analysis than to any physical tiredness. Today it was a cross current that required answers. A narrow band of ripples bisected the calm bay. Light started jumping. There was an airborne hiss, followed by the laughing noise of water on hull. Suddenly my horizon fell under the influence of a sideways drift. The tide was roaring out and chose a spot miles from nowhere to exercise its surface rights. It was past suppertime before I made it to Roger Flower's fish cabin in Winsor Harbour. But as soon as my feet touched dry land I was treated to a fry-up of freshly caught arctic char.

' PREPARE TO MEET THY GOD'. I would like to meet the optimistic soul who painted that remark on a rock halfway round Cape Makkovik. Seriously, you keep a keen eye open for landmarks. There is nothing more infuriating than to pass a settlement after spending days dreaming about a hot bath and a night between clean sheets.

Forgive me, but I am a city kid. We are programmed from birth to stop at lights, cross at crossings, and to keep to the right. Nothing is left to the imagination. Not so on the Labrador coast. Here, there is no such thing as just one way; you are spoiled for choice. At the beginning of this trip, I had nightmares about rounding capes and dreaded crossing open bays, but island hopping I thought would be fun. Now, I have my doubts. Skylines can be a jigsaw puzzle of bumps, dots and lines when islands are thrown into the equation and with few standout landmarks to follow, plotting the right course between them can be like threading the eye of a needle.

Rigolet had its Narrows to go through. Makkovik was second left past Cape Strawberry, and Postville had only one entrance that even a blind man could follow down Kaipoko Bay. But searching for Hopedale through a maze of islands would prove a major headache.

Navigating Kanairiktok Bay from Winsor Harbour to Flagstaff Tickle started on the wrong foot. Two islands I was heading for slowly became one. Then to compound the error, a large island I had taken bearings from drifted apart into two. Either I must have drunk extra strong coffee that morning or someone had slipped something into my tobacco. Whatever the reason, the horizon just didn't read right. Islands were in clusters and mostly barren. The only difference today was that they appeared to be hanging in the sky above the horizon. It was one of those clammy days, hot, still and sweaty. Distances were an illusion and was speed anyone's guess. It took four hours of course correction to cross Kanairiktok Bay and if I thought the worst was behind me, I had more of the same down Hopedale Run.

The wind picked up near Flagstaff and dark clouds formed like mothballs. Glass calm turned into swells and with strong cross currents to contend with and I found the kayak surfing one minute and crashing through waves the next. The sun had long ago lost its heat and my fingers were numb. I should have stopped, made camp and called it a day but I couldn't get those clean sheets of Hopedale out of my mind.

Just past Flagstaff Tickle, I nipped behind a small rocky island for a rest, only to reappear ten minutes later, completely lost. A fine mist cloaked my view. All silhouettes blended into one and I was half way down Deep Inlet before realizing my mistake.

There is nothing more strength-sapping then realizing you have just added six miles to your day's work, especially if they are a twin of yesterday's fiasco. It wasn't until I stopped to climb a hill and saw Hopedale's red and white radio antenna that I realized I was back on track.

By 7:30 p.m. I was limping into harbour. I'd been paddling for ten hours. The fine mist was becoming a steady downpour and above, clouds were queuing up for their evening dump. Then, just as if to rub salt into the days wounds, I had an embarrassing welcome.

I saw a dozen people waving in my direction from the wharf. My spirits soared. I was soaked, very cold and dog tired, but they gave me a second wind. I put on a sprint, but no sooner had I come within hailing distance when Bertie Winters in his long liner 'Viola Dee' passed. They'd come to see Bertie, not me, and no sooner had he docked than backs turned. I was left to come in unnoticed, so much for celebrity status.

It was a classic example of the saying, 'Sometimes it is better to risk and conquer the elements then be conquered by them'. Some consolation. My body screamed out for warmth. I had no control over my fingers and unpacking the kayak was an exercise in futility. Thankfully, I didn't have to struggle long. Roger Flowers had hitched a lift on the Viola Dee and seen my arrival. He made arrangements for me to stay with his father, Chesley. I was suffering a mild touch of hypothermia, but a quick shower worked wonders and my bottomless appetite recovered just in time to devour a meal of fried seal meat.

There is a very real pain in Labrador. Maybe that's what humbles. Whether it's the physical pain of a good hard day's work, the constant battle with nature, or its isolation, it's not for me to judge. One thing I can say; it made nights like this, the tea I took to my bed and the food resting in my stomach that much sweeter.

Was I dreaming? Had I woken up in Egypt? What jumped into my vision wouldn't have looked out of place next to the Sphinx. Whoever coined the term 'PYRAMID OF WOOD' must have had George Flowers in mind. It was humongous. It made every other pyramid on the coast look like a puny wigwam. Most people cut and season a winter supply of logs and pyramid another year's supply of sticks if they feel energetic. George is either the world's biggest hoarder of wood or else he knows something about the 'End of time Prophecies' we mere mortals don't.

Everything about Hopedale wreaks of character; its location, a blend of beauty and the beast, dotted with picturesque coves and jagged rock; its majestic backdrop of mountains and bottomless bays cut deep like mortal wounds. It's the sum total of poetic license and wild fantasy. Hopedale, I was told, was last on the list for almost all amenities. Built on granite rock, water and sewer services are still in their infancy. The cost of blasting and burying pipes is steep. Manhattan may have its bedrock, its skyscrapers and Times Square, but it also has the clout and money to blast its way into the 21st century. Hopedale has neither, but there lies its attraction. What government can't exploit, it leaves alone.

"CATCH!"

I had walked into Hopedale's answer to 'Cincinatti's Riverfront Stadium' with one major dif-

ference. Its field wasn't built on the banks of a river,
but either side of one. A stream cut between first base
and home plate and while I watched, a fielder
jumped in up to his ankles to make a catch. With a
field full of holes, water traps and boulders, it took a
braver man than myself to play on it. Right field was
bordered by the new nursing station, left field by the
variety store and centre field could be any one of
three kitchen windows. You had to be fleet of foot to
run the bases and double-jointed to field a ground
ball. I did see someone slide into base, but he got up
limping. In short, to be an average fast ball player in
Hopedale, you had to be able to bat, run, catch, jump,
swim and have eyes in the back of your head to
dodge the mosquitoes. It makes no wonder that ath-
letes here are as hard as the rock they play on. I even
heard of a golf course being built, but then that was
only a vicious rumour put around by a local official
gunning for a make-work program.

By day three I was getting worried. My wrists still
made grating sounds and the tips of my fingers were
still alienated from the rest. I hate giving in to doctors. I am not a happy camper when told to rest and
can't abide taking pills. I was brought up in the era
when nature was its own nurse and good wholesome
exercise was the great remedy. But pain is pain and it
wouldn't go away.

The Grenfells are an institution on the coast.
Founded by their namesake, its doctors and nurses
are a mixed bunch of missionary zealots, high tech
runaways and free-spirited adventurers. There are
no live-in doctors on the coast. Broken legs, child
births and patients needing surgery are flown either
to Goose Bay or St. Anthony, Nfld. for treatment.
What's left falls to the Grenfell nurses to administer.
They are a jack-of-all-trades, combining the need for
a bandaid dispenser, faith healer, and a shoulder to
cry on. You name it, they do it.

From Mary's Harbour to Makkovik, I had always
made a point of visiting the nursing station when in

town. I liked socializing with them. Sometimes it was just for a chat and a cup of tea; sometimes a three course meal, and sometimes to check out their shapely curves, but today it was all business. Miss Ann McElligott was from the old school, a no-nonsense nurse with a warm personality that both age and self-confidence breeds. She didn't short-change me with pain killers or fog me with science. I left with a wrist support bandage, a plain old 'give it some rest' prescription and a warm smile. It worked wonders and by the end of the next day I felt confident enough to continue.

I had one more visit before I called it quits. Bertie Winters had just returned from Windy Tickle and was down by the wharf loading up with salmon en route to Makkovik. Without the likes of Bertie, there'd be no salmon industry. He covered the outposts from Cape Harrison in the south to Windy Tickle in the north and come rain or shine, Bertie's long liner, Viola Dee, is the boat that picks up the salmon and delivers it to the fish plant in Makkovik for processing. He is a major link in the chain that gets fish from the sea to the kitchen table. I wanted to pick his brains on the coast ahead, but most of all I just wanted to meet him.

Bertie is built like a stick of chewing gum. Sat in his wheel house, he wouldn't have looked out of place as Bogey's stand-in on the 'African Queen'. Like so many others of his generation, words were for socializing. You learned by experience or not at all, so advice came only after persistent prodding. I was still halfway down the evolutionary scale when it came to seamanship, so I was all ears. Everything about the man blended in with the fishing images I'd formed in Goose Bay and listening to him talk about the coves and safe harbours ahead, especially their names, his affection with, or contempt for, put life into the likes of Snug Harbour and Cut Throat Island. He left no room for excuses. You finish what you start, that was his motto. Nain, he said, would be no problem.

Windy Tickle would be windy and Big Bay would be big. I got all caught up in the romance of it and by the time Bertie left, anything seemed possible.

Chapter 20
A Rare Moment of Sea Harvest

MAPS SOMETIMES OFFER SURPRISING insights into the cultural landscape. Yesterday the Islands read in English, today Innuktuk. I was now travelling in Innu and Inuit country and not only was its rich heritage reflected in tongue-twisting names like Akpiktok and Napatalik, but also in its scenery. Everything looked larger than life; the wall of rock on the run up Windy Tickle, its wild contours, depth of field and its amazing shades of blue. Even man-made beacons captured the spotlight. Cape Harrigan's civil defense radar site dominated the sea lanes. Built like a futuristic fortress, its white dome's location wasn't on any map I knew of and that wasn't the only landmark missing. Huge rocks, shoal and sandbars often appeared where they weren't shown. Bay of Islands was a prime example - a swell bottomed out on rocks in the middle of nowhere. They weren't death traps to a kayak, but each incident sent me back to the drawing board.

It was turning out to be another average day of calm weather when the wind struck, clouds stretched, closed ranks and flew big time. It all happened with lightening speed. Strong gusts cut broad furrows. Surface water foamed,took off, then carried like white smoke. I didn't so much call it quits as get blown ashore. I beached on the gravel bar on Napatalik Island, but as sooner as the tent was erect, the wind died.

'IS THERE ANYBODY OUT THERE?' As I've said before, I'm not religious by a long shot, but there are times, and tonight was one of them, when life skips onto another plane. Call it fate or just plain luck that blew me where it did. By all accounts, I should

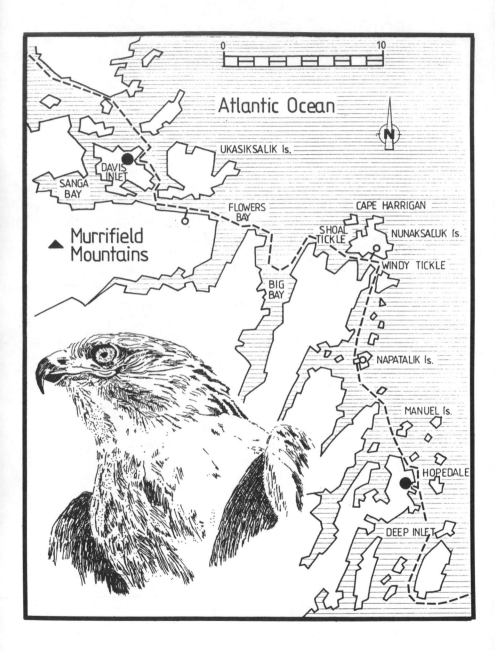

have been tucked away for the night in a fish cabin down Windy Tickle. Instead, I was outside. It was one of those glorious nights. A touch of frost kept the mosquitoes quiet. I could sit outside in peace and watch the sky go technicolour. Blood reds changed into deep purple then into the ink-black cloak of night. It was a childhood fantasy come true. My own observatory. The night sky was crystal clear. I traced the Big Dipper, found the North Star and lined in the likes of Scorpio, Aries and Taurus the Bull. I must have tracked half a dozen satellites, named three planets and gazed in wonder at the Milky Way before the main event started. It began with a distant glow, like the far off haze of city lights. It slipped over the mountains, grew in brightness then exploded with life. Lines, tails, curls. It was everywhere. A curtain one minute, an old man's whiskers the next. It went from white to fluorescent green, then to dull amber. For two hours the Northern Lights gave me a show the likes of which I had never experienced before. I was in seventh heaven when the deep dull base tones of an engine's heart beat earthed me. For fifteen minutes, I scanned the darkness, listened and waited, then a Christmas tree of lights appeared. It slipped into view from nowhere, moved effortlessly in my direction, answered my waves with a blast of steam then slowly beat its course south. It was the 'Petro Can' en route to Hopedale and its quarterly top-up of diesel for the thirsty hydro storage tanks. The tanker brought with it the key for tomorrow's passage. Windy Tickle hides its opening well, but Petro Can opened it. I set the bearing to memory, turned back to the tent and was soon lulled to sleep by the muffled groans of a grounded iceberg.

The word tickle originates in the description of a body of water between Islands or the mainland where the passage is so narrow that it tickles the sides of a boat. So much for dictionary terms. In reality, I found myself the next day sandwiched in a three way tie, with the narrow waters of Windy Tickle a stone's throw away. It was no contest. The speed boat left all in its wake and no sooner had its tail of spray disappeared behind the jaws of rock than the Taverner passed on cruise control. I'd been spotted. Decks filled, cameras shot and the boat rocked to the sight and sounds of waving excitement. It was rush hour on the high seas and the tickle only acted as an echo chamber to their welcome.

Put together a two mile wall of solid rock, a half mile corridor of water, a strong north easterly and you've got action. It was a day for surfing. The current and wind were in opposition and to say the waves were tickling my hull was an understatement. I was being tossed every which way but forward. Yet Windy Tickle was the easy part; the 90 deg. turn into Shoal Tickle was serious business

What is it about 'T' junctions that attract accidents? Stop, go, right, left. If I could have beached, I would have, but there were no toe holds. The turn into Shoal Tickle was a nightmare. The wind was relentless. Waves crested, washed over waist high and gave my cockpit's waterproof skirt a rare workout. Having said that, the kayak never once wobbled. The rudder worked wonders. I was able to set a diagonal course to Nunaksaluk Island and let my hips do the rest. Two hours later, my nasal passages were being massaged by the smoke of a black berry root.

You could be forgiven for mistaking a smoke house for an outside toilet. At first I thought it was occupied by a chain smoker, but there was no mistaking the smoked char I dined on that evening with the Broomfields, its distinctive taste, its crunchy texture and its entrapped juices. Awful good, boy!

The next day I had the most amazing experience. It was one of those rare moments of sea harvest the National Geographic loves to cover and one your average tourist can only dream about. It was not so long ago that hunting of whales and seals was an essential ingredient of Labrador life. Their meat was a rich source of protein and their blubber, when turned into oil, an excellent substitute for fire lighter. Times have changed. We are now living in an age of Greenpeace. Now, today's hunters are more likely to be armed with a camera and shoot through the eye of a lens than your standard 303. Animal rights may be a dirty word on the coast, but their sympathizers are numerous and their access to the all-powerful southern media a much easier sell for them than your average Labradorian rifle owner. Personally I came north to eat game, not to photograph it, but after today I may change my mind. My first whale sighting came down Kaipkoko Bay and by Winsor Harbour, whales had become an everyday part of my trip. They came in singles, pairs and in pods numbering as many as six. I spotted them rounding Capes on calm days, swimming against the currents, down narrow tickles and, like today, down Big Bay. All these sightings had the same calling card - a noisy whoosh - then silence. There are only a few documented cases of collisions at sea, but to my mind one accident is one too many. Whale watching may be a safe pastime from a speed boat, but I can do without that unwanted adrenalin rush from within a kayak. Thank God they are slow and predictable. Like a train trapped on lines, the only time they are going to strike is if you suffer from suicidal tendencies or if, like today, you pass over their food chain.

I had the first hint of the day's treat while paddling down Shoal Tickle. Dead caplin were everywhere. I found them washed up on rocks and marking the high tide on beaches. They were coming ashore to spawn and that meant a feast day for every seal and whale in the neighbourhood.

There is an old saying, 'Man can't live on bread alone and sex won't fill an empty stomach!' When I first arrived on the coast, I thought the fresh air and high sperm counts were the reasons for large families. I never thought about the diet until I started to eat fish. I have tasted smelt, trout, arctic char, salmon and rock cod, but caplin are in a league of their own. Deep fried in flour, roasted or just plain dried, they are a meal in themselves, so who could blame me for taking time out to go sightseeing?

I arrived at the mouth of Big Bay just as the tide turned. The sea was calm and there wasn't a hint of clouds in the sky. Underwater, rocks rushed up to meet me like mountains. Paddling shoal water on calm days is akin to low level flying. Sea life viewed through clear salt water magnifies its quality. Pebbles look like rocks and trout like trophy salmon. For thirty minutes, I drifted through this scene, then suddenly the curtain dropped. It was caplin, millions of them. A liquid pool of black on amber.

It didn't take long for the news to spread. A school of seals appeared, then a pod of whales. I couldn't have orchestrated the events better. I was right in the middle of the action and while seals swam towards me, whales circled just off the shoal.

The seals struck first. One moment a dozen heads bobbed up and the next a thousand bubbles exploded underneath. Instant pandemonium, a flipper, blurred outlines and caplin shooting off in all directions. It was a case of survival of the fittest without table manners, an eating frenzy that passed within seconds. Moments later the pod surfaced, then a lone seal only feet from the kayak. It was an old square flipper. A large grey, with cat-like whiskers and puppy-dog eyes. I was on top of it immediately. Suddenly his whole boy arched, snapped back like an elastic chord and crashed back under the surface. I'd been spotted and the noise set off a chain reaction. Moments later caplin were jumping and the whole scene replayed itself as seals rushed in for the kill.

It didn't end there. I was just turning for shore when a thundering roar had me staring down a grampus. Who can be scared when a huge whale arcs out of the water belly up? It was amazing. First one then another grampus roared to the surface. Caplin were everywhere and those which escaped the jaws of the whales and seals were eagerly awaited by scores of scavenging gulls lining the shore.

I was now on the tail end of my trip and today's experience was just icing on the cake. To an outsider like myself, sightings of game, whether it was a whale or jay, punctuated many a lonely day. I could count on the osprey down Lake Melville and ranger seals near Smokey. Large companies of drakes, eider and guillemots were always following my progress. Even terns dropped in, following strong easterlies. Then there was the day a lone mosquito hitched a lift, left momentarily only to return with reinforcements. And what about the time I paddled into thousands of puffins, who splattered me with ....OOPS!, well that's another story.

The day ended quickly. A decorated beach of driftwood, a brook of cool ice water and a sheltered campsite. I lit a huge bonfire, smoked out the mosquitoes, then sat back into my appetite. Fire, water and shelter a trilogy for a nomad. After eight months, I wore its collective parts like a second skin. It had the brand of a rolling stone and would take more than a scrub down to wash off its ingrained rhythms.

That night the heavens rained light. A meteor shower lit up the sky like a laser show. Another lone night of wonderment, another epitaph for a travelling man. Once again I spoke to the invisible shadow, stroked that imaginary partner and fell into the hole of self-pity. Twelve years of travel add up to a lot of memories. I've lived the American dream, calypsoed my way through the Pacific and been bitten by the sights and sounds of Asia and Africa. I could write a book on the etiquette of hello and goodbye, and another on how to live out of a knap-sack. Over the years I have lost my roots to a multi-cultural mismatch. Labrador had awakened dormant feelings of belonging and that night I made a promise to give into its lure and add one more winter to my trip.

If ever there has been a people analyzed to death

it's the Innu of Davis Inlet. You can't put the genie back in the bottle. The white man is here to stay, but you sure can give them back the keys to their own future. I've never been a great believer of social contracts, spin doctors, or do-gooders. When all is said and done, if you're not master of your own destiny, then you're at the bottom of the ladder. Davis Inlet is quite literally built on the shifting sands of other people's ideas. Only the day before, I had crossed paths with a group of Innu returning by speed boat from a duck hunt down Flower's Bay. Impish laughter followed my every gesture and curious eyes my equipment. Today in Davis, my welcoming committee was a combination of today's suspicion and yesterday's pride. I was an embarrassment, somebody else's problem that happened to paddle in on the morning tide. I had seen it all before in the eyes of displaced Bengali Tribal people in Asia, uprooted from their native forests, boxed, evangelized and tamed. I'd seen it again in the foothills of the Ruenzoris in Africa where a proud mountain people had been crushed by a Zaire government bent on mining. Call it evolution or submission or just the plain need of modern governments to make people into mirror images of themselves. It all comes under the umbrella of government relocation and the drug of subsidized handouts. Davis Inlet is just one more marginal community, no worse and no better than many searching for answers, and Ottawa is no closer to the mark than Dacca is in Bangladesh or Kinshaza in Zaire.

By late afternoon, I was ploughing through my first pizza in four months. Ken White, ex-teacher, local store owner and proprietor of one of the cosiest bed and breakfast establishments on the coast, had taken me under his wing. Ken is one of those 'come from always', a thoroughbred island man. Short and wiry, with a caustic tongue and razor sharp wit, you couldn't help but like him and fortunately for me it went both ways. You see, I was flying on an empty fuel tank. I'm not a great spender, but as any of my friends would tell you, I can't estimate myself out of a paper bag. I am the kind of guy who could win the lottery, turn up at the presentation and forget to bring the winning ticket. In this case it was an envelope containing a two hundred and fifty dollar money order left back in Mud Lake.

On the coast plastic money isn't worth the card it's printed on. American Express may have made inroads into the Gobi Desert, can be found down the Amazon and has climbed its way into the Himalayas, but they don't have offices on the north coast. Visa and Master Charge are still names of the future and your Diner Club Membership won't impress anyone at the local take-out. I could have brought my cheque book, but I found out too late. Government stores accept personal cheques and will cash them with the minimum I.D. To cut a long story short, I was financially embarrassed, and if it wasn't for Ken it could have been much worse.

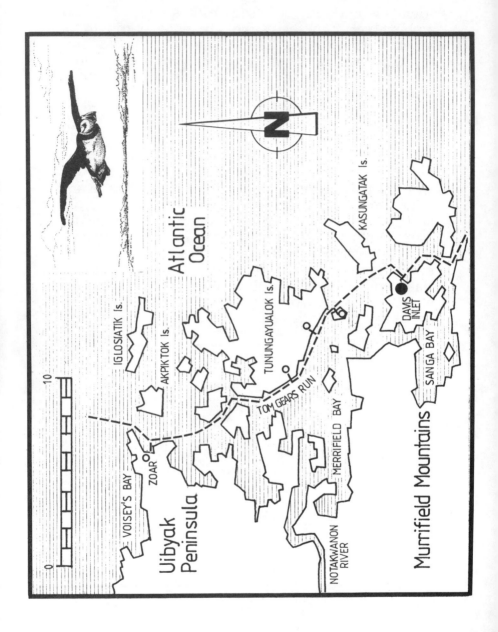

Chapter 21
The Final Chapter

AUGUST 7TH THE WEATHER FORECAST for Nain to Makkovik called for moderate north easterlies and overcast conditions with the chance of rain but - wait for it - an expected high of 4 deg. C. I can't remember what the low was, but who cares when the high is just above zero. It should have been too cold for the black flies, but the Labrador strain has blood as thick as lube oil. The air was alive with them. They hovered like dark halos above people and picked them off at random. Last night's rain must have incubated every egg on the coast and they were having a field day in Davis. My first mistake was to use the paddle for protection. Whack, splash. It's pretty hard to capsize in twelve inches of water, but not impossible.

It was an awful day for weather. The sky was scarred with dark layers and the air was pregnant with water. I should have stayed in bed but, once out, it was too late to crawl back.

The weather went from bad to worse. A prolonged squall blew me off course and the tidal sea currents carried me further. My maps showed a broken corridor of coastal islands from Davis Inlet to Nain. From here on it should have been plain sailing. There were no bays to cross, no exposed points to round and no breakers. All routes were sheltered, or so it seemed at first glance, but what it didn't show to the untrained eye was the influence these huge islands of rock would have on the conditions.

I kissed goodbye to plan one, an exploration of Sanga Bay, before even wetting my feet. Merrifield Bay, plan two, went before I let go of Iluikoyak Island and from that point onwards it was all up hill. By noon, the conditions had arrested my progress. I was

slipping past Kasungatak Island and towards the
open sea. And by mid afternoon I was paddling like
crazy against the thought of fog, sea lanes and collision with the Northern Ranger. It eventually rained
on cue. A flash of lightning, a roll of thunder and the
heavens opened.

The next day I made only six miles before calling
it quits on Tunungayualok Island. I was as sick as a
dog. The green lights of nausea hit before the first
tent pole was in place. Legs rooted, swayed, then
buckled. A mountain slid sideways, the sky arced,
then peace. I spent the night in contractions. My
whole body rattled like a bag of sticks and my head
was pounding.

What is it about mid-life crisis that drives your
average forty somethings on? MY EYES ARE FAIL-
ING, MY HAIRS TURNING GREY AND MY TEETH
ARE DROPPING OUT. I woke with a smoker's
cough, a retiree's bout of rheumatics, but still managed to drag my aching bones in the kayak.
Somehow, I punched a hole through cresting waves
and made four treacherous miles before admitting I
was sick.

It's difficult in the peak of health to steer an eigh-
teen foot kayak in heavy surf. Under normal conditions I would have continued to a safer campsite, but
I felt like death warmed up and couldn't cover another yard. I was heading for a quiet lagoon with a
sandy beach. The only problem was the half moon
barrier of shoal rock. The tide was in, but the deep
swells were exposing too many rocks for comfort. I
made one pass, spotted an opening and went for it.

The Beach Boys would have been proud of their
protege. I caught the big one and raced with it.
Everything was text book perfect; my side brace,
weight displacement, and steering. Then the bottom
fell out of the wave.

Imagine a trainee truck driver thrown in at the
deep end, told to reverse at speed while rounding

obstacles. That's how it felt when the swell sucked me back, spun the kayak sideways and deposited me behind an exposed rock. What happened next is a blur of pain. The wave was all noise, the movement quick and the action of being raised forward, up, over and backwards, muscle-popping. It would have been better to capsize behind the rock, but I am not good at second guessing. The strain of bending and twisting two ways in a split second wrenched my back. It went from poker hot to dull ache and by the time I beached it felt like a twisted rod.

The next morning my spine was locked in a hideous curve of pain. I couldn't stand straight without thoughts of passing out. Sudden movements triggered shock waves, left me breathless, light-headed and dizzy. The previous 48 hours had sobered me up. Illness is an unwanted bed fellow at anytime, but doubly so when visited on without warning. My prediction of reaching Nain in two days had evaporated. I was still within hailing distance of Davis Inlet. One week would be a closer guess, and if my back got worse my trip might end before Zoar. I could find no enjoyment in the weather either. You didn't have to be a climatologist to work out the signs; wispy clouds, erratic squalls and a hazy sun, they had all the hallmarks of a full blown storm. I had three options: stay, go back or go forward. I didn't fancy staying; storms have a bad habit of outstaying their welcome. The thought of hanging round for days or of returning to Davis was almost as painful as my back. Once again it was mind over matter. I broke camp in slow motion, packed loosely and took an eternity to drag my kayak into the water. Thankfully the pain left when I sat down.

Tom Gears Run was done very slowly. I was just going through the motions when the sun broke free. Slowly the heat worked its miracle and when the current took over and my kayak took off, life was on an upswing. At Gibraltar Island, I turned due North to

Zoar and straight into some welcome comic relief.
"Hello Boy."

I was just about to acknowledge the lone hailer
when his boat burst into life. Six heads popped up,
closely followed by forty eight sticky fingers. They
had enough cases of Pepsi, crisps and chocolate bars
to keep a cinema full of teeny boppers through a
weekend of midnight madness. They were dumb-
struck. Eyes as big as saucepans looked into my face.
My hair, uncut and unkempt, must have looked more
like the knotted dreadlocks of a rastapharian than
your average short back and sides of coastal norms,
and as for my dark brown eyes, they now had that
bloodshot 24 hour yeast high look about them. With
all the coastal hype about AIDS, lung cancer and
world starvation, who could blame the children's
stares? To most pre-teens, television is the only window of information on the outside world. True, there
are many whites living above the sixty first parallel,
but not many paddling a bright yellow kayak, with a
skin colour to match. We exchanged the usual greeting, asked those predictable questions, then a pure
gem fell from my friend's lips. Zoar was hidden by a
shallow point and its gravel bar made me uncertain
of my position.

"What's round the next point?" I asked. There was
a long pause. Eyes passed from the sea to the children, to me and back to the sea again.

"More water, boy."

I fell into that one.

"More water, there's water all the way to Nain.
It's been that ways as long as I can remember."

I reached the two-cabin summer harbour called
Zoar just ahead of the day's storm. The bottom had
fallen out of the barometer and two fronts were on a
collision course. Above, two dark lines stretched for
as far as the eye could see; two armies rushing to
battle at 20,000 feet. Below, the graveyard shift was in
full flight. A flock of black ducks screamed past knee
high, then another. Sea gulls had long since retreated

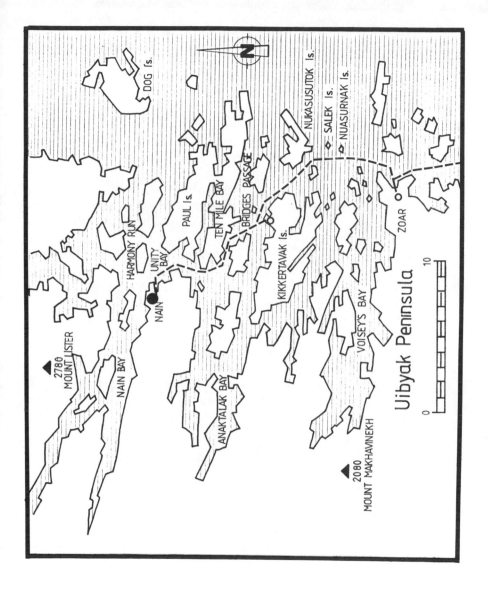

inland and seals to the safer waters of the off-shore
ice flows. A dark curtain of rain rushed in from the
east, calm waters turned to white caps and the first
blobs of rain overtook me on shore. By the time I had
unpacked, soothed my back against a cabin fire and
swallowed my first spoonful of stew, it was blowing
a gale. This was a Labrador hurricane. Sheets of rain
bounced off rocks and instant streams were springing
up around every crevice. Rain turned to hail, back to
rain, then to hail again. It searched out cracks, tested
joints and streaked the windows with eddies of
water. Inside, a warm fire was crackling. The walls
echoed with the sounds of country and western and
its shelves, full of exotic book titles, held the keys to
dreamland. I should have been counting my blessings. The Murrays were more than hospitable about
my intrusion. The smoke from their home had raised
my spirits and its lighthouse style top had beaconed
my way into harbour. It was bliss to be inside, only
my stomach complained.

Seals intestines may be an edible protein par
excellence, but to my eyes they look no more and no
less than rubbery links of chain and try as I could, my
brain would not mask its message. I've eaten some
strange things in my time. Sheeps eyes are a delicacy
in New Zealand and fried snake an everyday appe-
tizer in Indonesia. I've eaten roasted cockroaches in
Uganda and curried goat brains in India, but the sight
of stewed seal intestines wasn't exactly what I'd
planned on after a hard day's paddle. My stomach
started to rumble before the first slivers touched my
lips and by the time I swallowed the first chunk my
whole body had picked up on the chorus.

Chesley Flowers at 80 is a living example of a seal
diet and he swears by it. He is built like a pocket bat-
tleship, with 'full sized' shoulders and hands like
sledge hammers, so who was I to question his habits?
Under his roof in Hopedale, I was treated to daily
doses of dried, fried and boiled seal. It lit fire crack-
ers in my blood, turned up my toes in minutes and

gave me an adrenalin boost that lasted all the way to the toilet. I just couldn't keep it in and, try as I might, no sooner had it passed down one orifice than it was streaming out through another. I just couldn't get used to its rich taste or its high protein level. During mealtime at the Murrays I picked around the corners, searched out the onions and prayed that what lay below the surface was rice, not meat.

For two days the storm hammered at the door, then on the third night the clouds emptied. Tomorrow's coastline rose in leaps and bounds. Huge buttresses of rock cut into the sunset. Sharp, colourful outlines turned into a ghostly blue mist, then black on blue before losing themselves into a ragged edge of black. Soon, stars filled the sky and once again the sea was at rest.

I was off and paddling at the crack of dawn, but I wasn't alone. For thirty minutes I was circled by a whale. For once, I was the main attraction, the viewed not the viewer, and it was a strange experience. The whale sunk effortlessly, would be lost from sight for minutes, then surface with its patented calling card, the air spout. Twice it came within spitting distance and once I was sure I could see its dark shadow pass directly underneath. Four times it circled. Was it checking me out? Trying to make cosmic contact? Who cares, a whale is a whale is a whale. It was my twentieth sighting in as many days.

I was on the crest of a wave. My back had been anaesthetized by the morning's sun and the beauty ahead was unreal. A blue haze of mountains topped in sparkling white. Hidden inlets, open spaces of reflection and always the rhythmic sounds of rushing water over pebbles when beached. Here and there patchwork quilts of blues and yellows fought for life and you couldn't beat their ever-present corridors of flowery scent.

I hoped to make Nain that day, but gave up within sight of Taktok Bluff. Waves always look more threatening coming than going. The tide had changed and so had the surface. Thirty minutes before, the swells had been with me and I had surfed them with ease. Now they crested, rocking me in their cradle and stripping me of strength. I was swinging around like a kite in the wind and was lucky to find a sheltered sand bar when I did.

The sun set into a deep blue, then violet, mist. It was my last night and I wanted to savour it. Tomorrow was put on hold. I emptied my thoughts, lay back in the moss and let the purple drifts of the northern lights wash over me.

Frost! I woke to a crisp crust. Autumn had arrived early and its razor sharp wind underlined the fact. Labrador was in transition. I was being tested with a final change of seasons and all morning my body temperature dropped through the thermometer. I made the first pit stop of the day behind Sentinal Hill, lit a fire and had a brew-up. My fingers were numb and my face was chapped from the wind yet the weather only got worse. Bridge's Passage pounded me with surf. The sky looked wild and the landscape a twisted vision of hell. If I could have escaped down Ten Mile Bay I would have, but its entrance was blocked with a thunderous wall of sound. I was now hugging the contours of South Channel Cairn. The mountain of rock acted as a wind break, but when its point came into view my heart dropped.

Why does the worst weather always save itself for the last lap? I rounded the point only to meet a wall of cresting waves. An unstoppable air flow ran smack up against an unmoveable tide - sum total, chaos. I was bouncing about like a rubber boat in a bath tub. I could see Nain at the bottom of Unity Bay, almost touch it. I could make out the wharf and the white picturesque church and its stretched-out community of box-shaped houses. I could even make out movement, but the only sounds came from the wind and surf. After two months of kayaking, I should have bccn fit, but I felt like a shell of a man. I was paddling like crazy just to stay still. If I didn't get away from the point soon, my exhaustion would end up broken on the rocks and if I didn't make headway into the bay either, the running tide of breakers would pull my shoulders apart. I never doubted for one moment I'd get there, but I didn't want to retreat round the point and wait for the tide and wind to agree. The thought of a six pack, a soft pillow and a fresh caribou steak was too good to let go. For the last time, I locked onto my subject, shut down my mind and gunned it. Twice, speed boats came within hailing distance. I had visions of shredded flesh. Neither saw me; how could they? Spray was everywhere. It was a crazy end to a journey full of incidents but I would have been disappointed with anything less.

Chapter 22
Party Time

Ten hours ago I was sober. Then the drink came out. It was time for some heavy-duty partying. Time to talk about my eskimo rolls, the iceberg that nearly chopped me in two and the killer whale that stalked me for hours. At times like these a good lie is better than a dull truth and as the night slipped into overdrive their quality got better and better. It's now 5:30a.m. The sun rose before my head hit the sack. Deano's house resembles a battlefield and a thick fog smudges its corners. Above the ceiling hangs from the floor and the walls are swaying. Objects started to blur after three hours of drinking; after five, I threw in the towel and began nursing mugs of coffee. I think I am now lying on the living room couch but I couldn't swear to it. My body's suspended and my brain fried. The sounds of Ozzie's nasal passages resemble the rumblings of a passing freight train and Bev's constant chatter, the background hum of a spectator sport, in full cry. Wine can do that to you, but beer and wine most certainly will. It's just another day in the life of Bernie with one exception, the **'JOURNEY THROUGH LABRADOR'** is finished.

I paddled into Nain on August 14th. I had been on the road, so to speak, for 200 days and it slipped by all too quickly. The flabby city kid has turned into a lean, mean travelling machine. My 'Pee Wee Herman' looks have changed into those of 'Arnie the Swartz'. I've developed biceps the size of footballs and pectorals that would be the envy of most women. In short, I have found the fountain of youth: pain, pain and more pain. I have shrunk that middle-age bulge and in the process increased my hormone count. But I digress. Allow me to back peddle somewhat and give you a flavour of camp life in Mud Lake and the party to end all parties.

I returned from Nain to Goose Bay in the middle of August. My departure to Toronto has been put on the back burner indefinitely. Mud Lake had got under my skin and its people in particular.

I slipped back into the routine of village life like an old sock. There were friends to visit, a camp site to be found and wood to be collected for a winter stay. Uncle Tom, Mud Lake's answer to the bionic man, got me started in the back channel. We cleared some willows, chopped down a few young spruce and erected two canvas tents. I spent the next two weeks scavenging floor boards, begging, borrowing and stealing used insulation, installing two tent stoves, yards of flue pipe and one oval shaped, Gerry Dyson special, bread oven. All through October I worked like a beaver, erecting pyramids of driftwood, buck-sawing and creating a make-shift woodshed and an out-house. Then disaster struck. I tried to boom three large trees down the Churchill River, got caught in its current, bent my kayak's rudder and, had I not beached on a sand bar, would still be floating down Lake Melville towards Rigolet. During this time, Bernie managed to stick an axe in his foot, carve up an index finger and get pinned under a falling tree. I was learning about camp life the hard way but enjoying every minute of it.

Freeze-up came on November 18th. One day open water, the next locked below three inches of ice. For thirty six hours Mud Lake was marooned from the outside world. Then a ski-doo trail was marked, an ice bridge formed and the Churchill River opened to traffic again. By December, I had exchanged the two and a half hour paddle to Goose Bay for groceries with a three hour walk, runners for snow shoes and kayak for sled. My neighbourhood caribou had left for the mountains and I was now woken by the coming and going of a none too friendly moose. I took the obligatory dip, following my axe head into cold water and nearly burnt my tent down twice. Shaunt was rumoured to have disappeared in a snow drift, and Ron 'hoppo' Hopkins to have gone for his yearly winter swim.

By Christmas my quarters were as cozy as any cabin and my social calendar consisted of burning the midnight oil, writing from 8:00 p.m. to 4:00 a.m. daily catnaps and overlapping visits to friends. It was just what the doctor ordered. I joined the darts league, became accustomed to losing Monopoly at Randy and Melissa's and enjoyed Herbert's wicked home brew. I could count on Gwen's endless cups of coffee to warm up the frigid days, Bud's silence and Chuck's regular midnight visits to fill the dead spaces between writing bouts. Salt pork fry-ups of caribou became a staple diet and pease pudding a meal in itself. Even my baking had improved from teeth-cracking burnt black to edible crusty brown.

Winter's lazy days stretched, then passed into spring before taking off into mosquito season. Summer finally arrived in June and I was just about to plan my cycle trip back to Toronto when Beverly jetted in. Young, attractive, unattached and intelligent, although that wasn't held against her, she bore the cross of being the Chaulk's youngest, and only daughter, with flying, if not cheeky, colours. You could see the hormones bounce. Rumours were rife. The betting was 2 to 1 that she had returned for Ozzie's good looks. Then there was the hairy long shot, the 2000 to 1 outsider from Britain. The bets were even that she had returned to spruce up on her mother's recipes before tying the knot with her boyfriend from Winnipeg, but the truth was that Aunt Tine wasn't too well and Bev was her favourite niece.

Individual experiences during a long trip like this one tend to run together like a water colour. It's hard to chose that 'Yeh Boy, I'm yours for the taking' kind of night. The one that wrong footed, stretched, teased and stood out in brilliant primary colours above the rest. People are what it's all about and Bev's leaving party brought together all my favourite ingredients : wine, women, FOOD and song. The party started slowly with a little male bonding, but by 8:00 p.m. the food had arrived, the women were seated and it was rock-em, sock-em time at Deano's. In attendance were the Chaulks, Raeburns, Michelins, Bests, Browns, McLeans, the four Dyson sisters out on good behaviour and a lone Howgate, spruced up and suitably fasted for the occasion. By 9:00 p.m. it was a touch of down and dirty sing-alongs with guitar picking Carl, but by 10:00 p.m. the songs had swung from modern to traditional and Uncle Austin was the picker of choice. Austin McLean may not be a household name outside Mud Lake, but God broke the mold after creating this man's deep brown, sandpaper voice. He may not have been able to rub up against the high notes any more, but his voice hadn't lost any of its emotional punch and he together with Alton Best, who surely in another life must have been a court musician, brought the house down with their heart-tugging renditions of 'May you never be alone like me', 'Mulligan's Bay' and 'High on a mountain on old Mokami. Gwen gave us all breathing space and silenced the party with her angelic voice. Then, 'Cool Dad' Maynard almost buried it with 'The Wild Wood Weed'. Midnight was celebrated with comic relief as Dean and Chuck, Hydro's finest, split the sound barrier and everyone's sides with their skit, 'Mississippi Garry' before disappearing on yet another bear run to the 'Valley'. By 4:00 a.m. the beers were running low and only the brave were left. Harry was into his Credence Clearwater Revival trip, while Ozzie was zinging off on one of his own. By 5:00 am. the sun had risen and the only singing came from the birds outside. By 6:00 a.m. only Cool Dad, yours truly, and Bev were in the land of the living, but by 6:30 am, Cool Dad had abandoned ship, Bernie had finally fallen prey to his biological clock and Bev had proved once again that youth and female guile wins out in the end.

Experiences like this are impossible on a time schedule. You can't plan them, they just happen. For your average visitor to Labrador, time tables can be prisons. Cocooned in speed, it's all too easy for them to capture images and leave believing that Labrador is just wilderness, whales and caribou. People are the name of the game. You can't share a drink with a carabou, talk to a whale, or make love to a sunset. For an orphan of travel like myself, evenings surrounded by friends like tonight is what life is all about.

I started this trip in the deep end, but with my eyes wide open. I have scratched the surface, got my hands dirty and, like that night, suffered the occasional hangover. I have had equal doses of good times and bad on this trip and this is how it should be. I am no saint. I have trodden on a few toes, burped and farted at the wrong times, but never outstayed my welcome, and hopefully left many more smiles than frowns.

On a scale of one to ten, Labrador is right up there with the best of them. True, there are few places to run and hide and it can be claustrophobic if you are a teenager with big dreams, or a person with money to burn and bright lights on your mind. That's on the negative side. On the positive, there is abundant fresh air, unfenced boundaries for children to explore, and smiles around every corner. It,s frontier with a capital 'F'. Men are still judged by the houses they build and women by their children.

I hope you have enjoyed reading this book as much as I have enjoyed seeing my name in print. Until the next time, 'BEAM ME UP, SCOTTY, OR SEND ME DOWN THE HOME BREW. Happy times are here again.